The Truth About English Grammar

The Truth About
English Grammar

GEOFFREY K. PULLUM

polity

Copyright © Geoffrey K. Pullum 2024

The right of Geoffrey K. Pullum to be identified as Author of this Work has been asserted in accordance with the UK Copyright, Designs and Patents Act 1988.

First published in 2024 by Polity Press

Polity Press
65 Bridge Street
Cambridge CB2 1UR, UK

Polity Press
111 River Street
Hoboken, NJ 07030, USA

ISBN-13: 978-1-5095-6054-7

A catalogue record for this book is available from the British Library.

Library of Congress Control Number: 2024934299

Typeset in 11 on 14pt Warnock Pro
by Fakenham Prepress Solutions, Fakenham, Norfolk NR21 8NL
Printed and bound in Great Britain by CPI Group (UK) Ltd, Croydon

The publisher has used its best endeavours to ensure that the URLs for external websites referred to in this book are correct and active at the time of going to press. However, the publisher has no responsibility for the websites and can make no guarantee that a site will remain live or that the content is or will remain appropriate.

Every effort has been made to trace all copyright holders, but if any have been overlooked the publisher will be pleased to include any necessary credits in any subsequent reprint or edition.

For further information on Polity, visit our website:
politybooks.com

Contents

Preface

If you have ever been led to believe that your grammar is bad, relax a little. This book aims to liberate you, not berate you. Its main aim is to lay out some of the most basic principles of grammar from the ground up, without presupposing any previous acquaintance, and to lay out those principles in a more modern and consistent way. But it also to some extent aims to free you from fears of accidentally violating grammar and being judged for it. Far too many alleged "grammatical errors" aren't mistakes at all: they presuppose rules that don't exist and never did.

I have little time for the people who bully others about their conception of "correctness," while purporting to be the guardians of the wisdom and beauty of the English language, especially when in fact they're doing little more than peddling traditional dogma and often getting it wrong. Sometimes they're really just objecting to a variety of English they dislike, or a development that's recent enough to be not what they're used to ("The awful way people talk today!"). There's often more than a hint of ethnic or class prejudice about their nose-wrinkling: they only really like the English used by people who grew up and went to school roughly when and where they did.

But worse, many previous grammar books frame even genuinely important rules in careless, false, or contradictory ways. Fuzzy generalizations and useless definitions are repeated in literally thousands of books. English grammar is too often treated as a body of entrenched dogma that should never be queried or revised. The traditional books tell us that nouns are naming words, verbs are action words, auxiliaries are helping verbs, adjectives are words that describe nouns, adverbs are words that describe verbs, pronouns are words used in place of nouns to avoid repetition, a preposition stands before a noun to relate it to another. . . None of these definitions really work. Anyone who takes them at face value and thinks about them is likely to assume grammar makes no sense.

I've been interested in the grammar of English since childhood. In 2002, I co-authored *The Cambridge Grammar of the English Language* (often called *CGEL*) with Rodney Huddleston. He showed me how much we need to break away from the ossified tradition of earlier centuries, and frame the description of the language in more coherent terms. *CGEL* does that, but it's a big fat reference work (1,860 pages) designed for specialists, preferably with some grounding in linguistics. This book is very different: it's aimed at people who have no prior experience with grammar but would like a modest-sized introduction to it that makes sense.

Leaving much of the traditional dogma behind won't make me popular with the writers of earlier books. Essentially all popular introductions, textbooks, and syllabi are stuck in the usual time warp, and their authors won't appreciate my ditching their terms and concepts.

The problem I'm pointing to – the reason I believe English grammar has to be stated in a new way – isn't that English changes over time. It does change, of course, but very slowly, without causing major problems. Books from a century ago are still fully understandable: young fans of the *Twilight* vampire stories (2005 onward) can read Bram Stoker's classic vampire story *Dracula* even though it was published more than a hundred years before they were born (1897). Even over a century or two, the changes in English grammar are fairly trivial – nearly as trivial as the grouses and grumbles about the way young people talk today.

Rather more serious is the problem of delusions about what the rules are: people simply will not look at what the evidence tells them. Simon Heffer says, "I happen to believe that the 'evidence' of how I see English written by others, including some other professional writers, is not something by which I wish to be influenced" (in the preface to *Strictly English*, 2010). This gives him no basis for his decisions other than personal peeves, reformist yearnings, or what he imagines follows from logic. What he dismisses is the only kind of evidence grammar can ever be based on: the facts of how English is actually spoken and written by the people we regard as competent in it.

I will not be indulging peeves or proposing bans here. I will try to present the truth about the grammar of English in an intelligible way, based on evidence from how real people speak and write – because if the rules of grammar are not ultimately founded on that, they have no rational basis at all.

The really crucial point, though, is not about the evidence. It's about the whole framework of definitions and assumptions people have been leaning on for 250 years. It needs revision. We need a framework of concepts based on modern thinking about how to describe grammatical systems. This does require the introduction of a bit of unfamiliar terminology, but nothing like what you need in order to master basic anatomy or chemistry. And you may discover that looking closely at the structure of the sentences of English is surprisingly interesting and rewarding.

Knowing something about grammar won't magically improve the quality of your writing; writing well does not emerge miraculously out of knowing some rules or definitions, but only from hard work and experience with trying to write sentences that will affect people the way you want to affect them. But knowing grammar will dramatically enhance your ability to see what the issues are, and understand the advice (whether good or bad) that more advanced books on grammar and usage and style present.

Many people have influenced this book, some more than they realize. Rodney Huddleston has always felt there should be an elementary book that explained why traditional English grammar needed revision, and I hope this book does some of that work. My friend Brett Reynolds, indispensable co-author of the 2nd edition of *A Student's Introduction to English Grammar*, has contributed hugely over the past decade, improving my understanding of grammar in a thousand ways. His matchless ability to spot both big-picture theoretical points and tiny points of detail enabled me to greatly improve an earlier draft. Ian Malcolm, my commissioning editor at Polity Press, caught other slips and made insightful suggestions for improvements.

A special acknowledgment goes to the copy editor who worked with me on the final typescript: Justin Dyer. Working with him was nothing like the usual experience of facing quibbles and objections and changes I didn't want. It was like working with a brilliant colleague who fully understood the project and helped me smooth out the final version and fix the last infelicities and inconsistencies. Justin doesn't just correct the misplayed notes, he hears the music in his head. I'm enormously grateful to him for making the completion of the book such a pleasure.

Last but certainly not least, I thank the grammarian I have shared my life with while writing this book: Joan Maling. Her sharp editorial eye has helped me to improve my writing for decades, but she is also a source of real linguistic wisdom, pointers to the literature, and ideas for illustrations. We see eye to eye on syntax as well as on life.

Notation guide

I use italics for example sentences and mentioned words; so I might write:

The word *the* is called the definite article.

I use bold occasionally for introduced technical terms; so I might write:

The word *the* is called the **definite article**.

I use small capitals for emphasized text. (They also appear in some column or row labels in table displays.) So I might write:

This has NEVER been true.

I use bold italics with a Capital Initial to make unique names for dictionary entries (they're called "lexemes" – I'll explain that in chapter 3); so I might write:

The lexeme ***Break*** has the forms *break, broke, broken,* and *breaking*.

The word ***That***$_{sbr}$ is a subordinator but the word ***That***$_{det}$ is a determinative.

As a way to signal that some sequence of words contravenes the rules of grammar, I use a strikeout line through the sentence. So I might illustrate a point about where you can put adverbs with these examples:

> *The police obviously know about it.*
> ~~*The obviously police know about it.*~~

The idea is to make it unmissable that the second one is not what anyone would normally write. The strikeout means that the second sentence has something seriously wrong with it in grammatical terms.

I will sometimes use one or two raised question marks to signal that a sentence sounds odd, or deeply weird:

> *?? Verdi was a composer and many operas were written by him.*

That's not completely ungrammatical, but hardly anyone would write like that (instead of saying *and he wrote many operas*). The weirdness really needs an explanation (and it gets it, in chapter 16).

Underlining is sometimes used simply to draw attention to part of a sentence: notice the interpolated phrase in *He must, for heaven's sake, have known.*

I try to avoid abbreviations, but for a few high-frequency terms they are very useful. The most important are these:

- I write **NP** for Noun Phrase (a phrase like *the quick brown fox* with a noun as its head or principal word).
- **VP** stands for Verb Phrase (a phrase like *jumps over the lazy dog* with a verb as its head).
- **PP** means Preposition Phrase (a phrase like *over the lazy dog* with a preposition as its head).
- **AdjP** means Adjective Phrase (a phrase like *too lazy* with an adjective as its head).
- **AdvP** means Adverb Phrase (a phrase like *so very quickly* with an adverb as its head).

1

Introduction

Most people seem to think that using a language is all about choosing **words**. It isn't. You could know every word in the dictionary and still not be able to say anything. You need to be able to form **sentences**. That means following grammatical rules. The **grammar** of a language is simply the system governing the way in which its sentences are put together. And different languages do it in different ways.

This book concentrates on how sentences are put together, not on words or their meanings and uses. It's not my job to tell you whether or not you should use the noun *impact* as a verb. My job is to make sure you know exactly what that means: what nouns and verbs are, and what roles they can (or cannot) play in sentences. Then you can decide whether to write *This could impact your life* (with *impact* as a verb) or *This could have an impact on your life* (with *impact* as a noun). Journalistic prose seems to use *will have an impact on the* three or four times as often as *will impact the*, but clearly both are in use by professional writers. It's your decision.

I find it really sad that so many well-educated English speakers are unable to trust their own judgment; they fear that their knowledge of grammar will betray them – that some ill-placed adverb or preposition or participle will expose them to ridicule. They imagine that rules of grammar are laid down in authoritative grammar books somewhere with the sole purpose of catching you out, and you have to obey them.

Sadder still, many such fears are mostly groundless. Certainly there are rules of English grammar – thousands of them, often highly tricky and complex to state – but users of English already obey most of the rules unconsciously. They draw on their tacit, internalized knowledge of English grammar every day whenever they speak, write, or understand anything. They couldn't say what the rules are explicitly, of course, any more than they could name all the bones in their hands, but their grasp of the rules is unconscious, almost like an instinct. We all make occasional slips of the tongue or the keyboard that we didn't intend, but mostly we know how to say things in English without much prompting.

Yet many people believe total falsehoods about grammar. They trust in rules they think they recall from some high school English class but couldn't state with any clarity now. What drives this strange phenomenon? Why should lifelong English speakers be afflicted by fear of nonexistent rules? It's mainly due to the existence of thousands of over-conservative usage books, how-to-write websites, and grammar-checking apps. Plenty of the material repeated in works by purported English grammar experts is just wrong. Their descriptions are clumsy, if not false, and the edicts and prohibitions they dispense are sometimes fictional.

I'm not saying there aren't any rules, and I'm not saying you can ignore the rules. There may be some creative writing teachers who are so liberally inclined that they say there are no rules at all about writing, but I don't think they can possibly mean it. Of course there are rules. Loads of rules. If I didn't follow the usual rules of English word order, then figure almost find I saying it out to impossible totally was what would you.

Let me repeat that last bit, this time obeying the rules of English: If I didn't follow the usual rules of English word order, then you would find it almost totally impossible to figure out what I was saying.

Those last fourteen words could be arranged in any of 87,178,291,200 different orders, hardly any of which are grammatically permitted. As far as I can see, only one correctly expresses the meaning I intended. Choosing any of the other 87,178,291,199 creates either some sort of error or else (in most cases) complete gibberish that no one could understand. So do not imagine I'm saying we can lighten up and ignore the rules. I'm saying we have to get straight on what the rules are.

Grammar and style

Knowing something about the grammar of the world's most important language (that's undeniably the status of English) can be useful for anyone. First, it's interesting to see something of the complexity of a system you have already largely mastered, but second, understanding grammar is fundamental for understanding advice about writing **style**. Style is a matter of making effective use of the possibilities that the grammar makes available. And you simply cannot talk about style, or set about criticizing it or improving it, without employing basic grammatical concepts. Grammar underlies style in the way that anatomy underlies fashion design: you couldn't become an expert at designing clothes without knowing that a typical human has arms, legs, elbows, knees, and feet.

What a grammar describes is not the qualities that define literary style. This book does not talk much about avoidable clichés, deprecated words, informal expressions, or weakness of rhetoric. That sort of thing, though appealing to many, is often highly subjective and influenced by passing fashions. Grammar is about the principles that determine whether some sequence of words is a sentence at all. The reason I've written this book is that for two or three centuries writers on the topic have analyzed grammar badly and explained it in antiquated, clunky, or totally mistaken ways. Confused dogma has been handed down from teacher to teacher since the 18th century, and repeated in books that often shamelessly plagiarize each other and repeat each other's mistakes.

It's an oft-repeated maxim that a truly experienced writer who understands style can risk breaking the rules. But I'm not talking about breaking rules. I'm interested in what the rules should say, and I'm warning you that most of the books on how to write English are loaded with supposed rules or prohibitions obeyed by nobody, whether expert or not. Take the case of the ridiculous advice, found in numerous books on how to write well, that you should avoid adjectives and adverbs. My point is not that when you're an established writer you can occasionally be allowed to risk the occasional adjective or adverb. I'm saying that the people who tell you not to use adjectives or adverbs in your writing are time-wasters and they don't know what they're talking about.

My plan is not to waste your time (which is why I've kept this book as short as I could). I will assume that you're serious about writing material in English that other people will read (that's obvious: if you're writing just for yourself, it simply won't matter how you write); that you haven't studied grammar in any depth before, so you aren't necessarily acquainted with all the technical terms grammarians use (I'll explain the ones I need simply, as and when they come up); and that you don't have endless hours to spend on the topic so you don't want arcane details, historical digressions, cutesy jokes, or childish cartoons.

What style you should adopt in your writing depends on who your intended readers might be. That I cannot know. You might be writing for an audience of one, like the teacher or professor who's going to grade your next term paper, or the editor of a magazine in which you're hoping to be published, or the boss for whom you have to write reports and memos. Or you might be writing for a small circle of fans on social media, or a few hundred readers of a blog, or the thousands of customers to whom you have to send business communications, or the millions of readers in the great wide world of literature who purchase your breakthrough debut novel. I won't make any assumptions about such things.

My task in this book is to tell you the truth about contemporary English grammar, rather than pass along the familiar old views of it that most grammar books repeat as if they were scripture.

Did you ever see the 1992 film *A Few Good Men*? There's a classic scene where the brutal Colonel Jessep (Jack Nicholson) has been ranting about what it takes to keep America safe, and is being needled under cross-examination by a prosecuting attorney (Tom Cruise) who demands that he should tell the court martial the truth. Jessep loses his temper and yells: "*You can't handle the truth!*" Well, I'm going to assume you can handle the truth.

Too much of what has been written about English is false, or at least two hundred years past its use-by date. For a long time the unreliability of the published literature on English grammar has needed a positive alternative that makes better sense. It horrifies me to see how bad most grammar books are. I feel like a biologist marooned in a world where most medical science books make no reference to the circulation of the blood, and show no awareness of bacteria or viruses. Because, make no mistake about it, if physicians were typically as incompetent in anatomy and biology as how-to-write books are in grammar, you'd probably be dead.

I mean that literally. The germ theory of disease hadn't even begun to take hold in 1800. People thought epidemics were caused by foul-smelling mists. The state of the art in grammar at that time was a million-selling book on English grammar by Lindley Murray (1795, heavily influenced by and sometimes plagiarized from Robert Lowth's *A Short Introduction to English Grammar*, 1762). During the 1800s, microbiological theories of what cause diseases emerged, thanks to heroes of science and medicine like Bassi, Koch, Lister, Pasteur, Schwann, and Semmelweis. Meanwhile in biology the theory of evolution by natural selection due to Darwin and Wallace began to make scientific sense of biology more generally. By 1900, biology and medicine were much more integrated, and both had changed beyond recognition. Yet grammar had made almost no progress. The same old stuff was still being parroted by schoolteachers everywhere – formulations dating from before Darwin was even born (1809).

It stops here. I won't be repeating any dogma from earlier centuries unless it is solidly confirmed as true and still holds today. Trust me.

Occasionally you may find yourself in the position of having to write for people who believe what they've read in those old grammar books, and perhaps have strong feelings about it. I argue in this book (with supporting evidence) that in many cases they are wrong. But you may need to be diplomatic, and phrase things the way somebody else wants them phrased. If your boss, teacher, professor, editor, or publisher insists that some form of words is wrong or ugly or illicit, you may have to write it their way. But I hope in such a circumstance you'll feel a lot better if you know both sides of the story. That is, it'll be easier to tolerate a boss who insists you mustn't ever write a passive clause if you know exactly what passives are. And it should give you a tiny bit of deep-down satisfaction to know that the boss is wrong about what constitutes bad writing – that you know more grammar than the boss does.

American and British English

I should make a brief remark, before we get down to the nitty-gritty, about the supposedly yawning chasm between American English (AmE) and British English (BrE). I've had decades of teaching experience in both America and Britain, and I'd say that few contrasts have been so grossly exaggerated. There are plenty of pronunciation differences, of course, and there are many words that are used one side of the Atlantic but not the other (BrE *lorry* for AmE *truck*, AmE *pitcher* for BrE *jug*, etc.). And spelling was long ago standardized in very slightly different ways. (I've decided to use AmE spelling in this book: see chapter 17.) But when it comes to grammar, the important thing to notice is how utterly trivial the differences are.

You'll occasionally notice a few contrasts in AmE and BrE speech. An AmE speaker is more likely to say *I did that already*, with the simple past *did*, in contexts where a BrE speaker would say *I've already done that*; but both understand what the other version means. A BrE speaker will sometimes answer a question with *She may do* where an AmE speaker would leave off the *do*; but intelligibility is not threatened. An AmE speaker will call 7:45 *a quarter of eight* while in BrE it's *a quarter to eight*, but they can still manage to meet for breakfast. For the most part, there weren't any AmE/BrE decisions to make when I was deciding how to frame the sentences in this book.

The idea that a few tiny differences in grammar and a sprinkling of different word choices could form a mighty barrier between cultures and worldviews is utterly ridiculous. Yes, Oscar Wilde said (in his 1887 short story "The Canterville Ghost") that "we have really everything in common with America nowadays, except, of course, language"; but he was JOKING! And yes, George Bernard Shaw said in various different ways that Britain and America were two nations separated by a common language, but that's nothing like a serious account of the facts.

The astonishing truth is that more than a billion people who use Standard English every day pretty much agree on sentence construction, down to fine details. British conservatives do grumble about "Americanisms" immigrating into BrE, but it's mostly down at the level of individual words. (The commerce goes two ways, incidentally: my friend Ben Yagoda runs a blog called *Not One-Off Britishisms*, devoted to curating a collection of BrE expressions that have crept into AmE.) The garments called pants in America are called trousers in Britain. But significant differences in the actual rules of grammar are as rare as hen's teeth. So let's start looking at grammar.

2

Clauses, sentences, and phrases

We start with the big units of language that can actually convey thoughts: clauses, which are the most important, then sentences, and then phrases.

Clauses

The primary concept in grammar is the **clause**. A clause is the smallest unit in any language that can express a complete thought or conversational contribution: a claim about what's true, or a description of some situation, or a question that seeks an answer, or an instruction that could be followed, or anything of that sort. A few examples of typical clauses will help to make this clear.

This stinks.
Sperm whales feed almost exclusively on squid.
What is cheese made from?
Cheese is made from milk.
What an idiot he was!
Get your hand off my leg.
whose body was never found
which he was looking at
whether she was aware of it or not
that he was cheating on her

Clauses in English can contain other clauses. Take the last two clauses above. You can tuck one inside the other, replacing *of it* by *that he was cheating on her*:

> *whether she was aware* [*that he was cheating on her*] *or not*

That's a clause about his cheating tucked inside a larger clause about her awareness. And the whole thing could be put inside an even larger clause: you could put *I wonder* at the beginning, for example.

Sentences

Sentences are larger units that can be uttered on their own to make complete conversational or narrative contributions. They are generally made up of clauses, either by tucking one clause inside another or by linking two or more clauses with a word like *and*.

Some teachers insist that a sentence MUST have the form of a clause, but if you read any literature at all you'll see that isn't true; but we can come back to that point.

Here's a fairly complex four-clause sentence, made up from the clauses listed above, which illustrates both embedding one clause inside another and linking two clauses together with *and*:

> *I doubt whether Moby-Dick would have liked cheese, because he was a sperm whale, and they feed almost exclusively on squid.*

This has a **main clause** (the one that isn't enclosed within any larger one) making a statement about my doubts. Within it is a clause raising a question for consideration: would Moby-Dick have liked cheese? After the word *because* comes a third clause, a statement about Moby-Dick being a sperm whale.

And after the word *and* comes yet another clause, an assertion about sperm whale food preferences. Here's the sentence again, this time with square brackets round each clause:

[[*I doubt* [*whether Moby-Dick would have liked cheese*]], *because* [*he was a sperm whale*], *and* [*they feed almost exclusively on squid*]].

What if we didn't have multi-clause sentences, so a sentence could only contain a single clause? The content of the sentence could be still be expressed, using four sentences each consisting of a single clause (though the effect isn't exactly the same):

Would Moby-Dick have liked cheese? I doubt it. He was a sperm whale. They feed almost exclusively on squid.

Phrases

Sentences also contain units called **phrases** (and actually we can regard a clause as just a special kind of phrase). Phrases can have any number of words, one or more, and can contain other phrases, but in each phrase one subpart is crucial, and is known as the **head**. Here are some of the phrases in the four clauses we just looked at, together with the labels that show what sort they are:

liked cheese: Verb Phrase (VP). The head verb is *liked*.
doubt it: Verb Phrase (VP). The head verb is *doubt*.
a sperm whale: Noun Phrase (NP). The head noun is *whale*.
was a sperm whale: Verb Phrase (VP). The head verb is *was*.
almost exclusively: Adverb Phrase (AdvP). The head adverb is *exclusively*.
on squid: Preposition Phrase (PP). The head preposition is *on*.
feed almost exclusively on squid: Verb Phrase (VP). The head verb is *feed*.

One particularly simple kind of clause contains an NP, which comes first and is referred to as the **subject**, and a VP, which completes the clause and is often called the **predicate**.

We'll need the term "subject" quite often in what follows, and I'll come back later to how it should be defined.

Heads and complements

There is always a **head** in a phrase. When it is not accompanied by anything else, we have a one-word phrase. *Cheese* can be an NP, and so can *squid*. If we didn't allow one-word phrases, we'd often have to say "either a noun or an NP," "either a verb or a VP," and so on. When I talk about a phrase, always remember that I DON'T mean a unit containing more than one word; I mean a unit with at least one word (the head), which MAY contain other words as well. The shortest sentence in the most familiar translation of the Bible (in John 11:35) is a one-clause sentence made up of a one-word subject NP plus a one-word predicate VP: *Jesus wept*.

The head in a phrase may require or permit the presence of another phrase such as an NP. Such an extra phrase, whether needed or allowed by a head word, is called a **complement**. Which head words take which complements is one of the most complex topics in grammar, because it involves the individual quirks and requirements of individual words, and there are tens of thousands of them. These examples illustrate just some of the possibilities (and I use bold italics for the words I mention, for a reason explained in chapter 3):

- The verb ***Dine*** cannot occur with a complement NP: ~~We dined pizza~~ is not grammatical but *We dined earlier* and *When do you usually dine?* ARE grammatical.
- The verb ***Eat*** PERMITS a complement NP, of the type known as a **direct object**, so *We ate pizza* is grammatical. But a

direct object is not strictly REQUIRED: *We ate earlier* and *When do you usually eat?* are also grammatical.

- The verb **Devour** requires a complement NP (a direct object), so *We devoured pizza* is grammatical but ~~We devoured earlier~~ and ~~When do you usually devour?~~ are not.

- The verb **Persuade** requires a complement NP (a direct object) optionally followed by a clause, as in *They persuaded the patient to stop smoking* or *They persuaded the patient that he should stop smoking*. The clause is not obligatory (we do find *They finally persuaded him*), but the object is required, so we don't get ~~They persuaded~~.

- Verbs like **Give** and **Hand** take two complements: the first is called an **indirect object**, and identifies a recipient or beneficiary, and the second is the direct object. **Give** allows both (*We gave them some money*), and either can sometimes be left out; but **Hand** strictly requires both: we get *I handed him the ticket* but not ~~I handed him~~ and not ~~I handed the ticket~~.

- Verbs like **Be** and **Feel** and **Seem** take a phrase called a **predicative complement**, often an adjective, as in *I felt vulnerable*. A predicative complement can be an NP, but it's very different from a direct object: *He seems a very nice guy* is roughly equivalent to *He seems very nice* (they both have predicative complements), but *He hired a very nice guy* isn't equivalent to ~~He hired very nice~~. That's because **Seem** takes a predicative complement, which may be either an NP or an Adjective Phrase (AdjP), but **Hire** must have an object, and an object has to be an NP.

- With the adjective **Proud**, a complement PP with the head preposition *of* is permitted but not required, so *She's proud of her army service* is grammatical but so is *She's proud*.

- With the adjective **Fond**, a complement PP with the head preposition *of* is required, so *She's fond of ice cream* is grammatical but ~~She's fond~~ is not.

It's tempting to think that the facts about which complements go with which head words are entirely explained by their meanings, but that's not true. It's not about meaning; it's about grammatical convention. But ideally a good dictionary should cover grammatical conventions of this kind: it should tell you for each word what sorts of complements it takes. Meaning will not suffice.

- **Shake** and **Quake** have basically the same meaning, and you could use either when talking about what happens in an earthquake, but *Shake the bottle* is grammatical and *Quake the bottle* isn't. That shows **Quake** does not take an object.
- **Likely** and **Probable** have no clear difference in meaning: *It's likely that she'll win* means the same as *It's probable that she'll win*. But *She is likely to resign* is grammatical while *She is probable to resign* is not. It's a fact about GRAMMAR (not meaning) that **Probable** doesn't allow a complement like *to resign*.

The requirements that particular head words place on their complements can be quite subtle. Take this example. The preposition **Out** permits a complement, which is normally a PP with the head preposition *of*, not an NP. So *I'm afraid you're out of luck* and *Don't try to get out of it* are grammatical but *I'm afraid you're out luck* and *Don't try to get out it* are definitely not. But **Out** can take an NP complement when the NP refers to a route of exit from an enclosed area, as in *The dogs ran right out the door* or *He threw the TV out the window*.

Adjuncts

In addition to heads and complements, the other parts of clauses are optional constituents called **adjuncts**. These can be **supplements**, which are interruptions of sentences that need to be separated off by commas (as in *The archbishop, a frail old man of 83, was visibly trembling*), or **modifiers**, which usually don't need flanking commas (as in *The normally courageous archbishop was visibly trembling*). In these examples the underlined phrases are all modifiers. Notice that any or all of them could be left out, and the result would in all cases still be fully grammatical and sensible sentences:

It came as a truly wonderful surprise.	[AdjP, modifying *surprise*]
I rather carelessly left the door unlocked.	[AdvP, modifying *left*]
We were hiding in the kitchen.	[PP, modifying *hiding*]
This became obvious the very next day.	[NP, modifying VP *became obvious*]
It's a plane she's never previously flown.	[clause, modifying *plane*]

3

Types of words

An Australian biologist named John Wilkins once made this shamefaced admission on his blog *Evolving Thoughts* (14 June 2008):

> I got through 12 years of state funded schooling with the sum total of my grammatical knowledge being – Nouns are thing words, verbs are doing words, and adjectives are describing words. I suspect we never covered adverbs.

Millions of people over the last three centuries have been taught what Wilkins was taught. And the feeble threesome of basic definitions he recalls is hopelessly inadequate. Words do come in different types, and I'm going to use the terms **noun**, **verb**, **adjective**, and **adverb** for four of them, but the definitions that Wilkins recalls are worthless.

Word-forms and lexemes

Before embarking on how words are divided into types, it is absolutely vital that we draw a technical distinction between two senses of the notion "word": one appropriate for doing word counts and the other more relevant to compiling a dictionary. How many different words are there in the following sentence?

He likes pampering you, and you like being pampered.

It would be entirely reasonable to say nine, or perhaps that eight different words occur but one of them appears twice. The words that appear once each would be *and, being, he, like, likes, pampered,* and *pampering,* and the word *you* appears twice. That's the right answer IF A WORD IS DEFINED AS A SEQUENCE OF LETTERS SEPARATED BY NON-LETTERS.

But a dictionary maker would object that there are really only six words here. You surely need only one entry for the verb *Like* in a dictionary: you don't include separate entries for *like* and *likes* – the *s* gets stuck on the end of *like* in certain contexts, and it's not the job of the dictionary to say exactly where; that's what the grammar is for. Similarly, *pampering* and *pampered* don't need entries; they can both be covered in the entry for *Pamper*. What's more, the word *being* would be covered in an entry headed *Be*. So the six words you need dictionary entries for are: *And, Be,* and *He* (one appearance each) and *Like, Pamper,* and *You* (each used twice).

For the second sense, where "word" means "item that should have its own dictionary entry," lexicographers sometimes use the term "lemma," but that has other meanings too, so among linguists the term **lexeme** is now standard, and I'll use it. For the different forms or shapes that belong to a lexeme we can use the term **word-form**.

And as a typographical convention, from now on I'll always put lexeme names in bold italics with a capital letter. So I'll say there is a lexeme called *Pamper*. It's the name of a small collection of word-forms with particular spellings – four of them: *pamper, pampered, pampering,* and *pampers*. I will always put word-forms (and all the phrases and clauses I mention as examples) in italics.

Let's go through the lexemes in the sentence about being pampered. In alphabetical order, they are: *And*, *Be*, *He*, *Like*, *Pamper*, and *You*.

- *And* has variant shapes in casual speech, sometimes indicated as *an'* or *'n'* by novelists, but otherwise there's not much difference between talking about the lexeme and talking about the word-form.
- *Be* is the extreme opposite – it has more distinct word-forms than any other lexeme. Its word-forms are: *be*, *been*, *being*, *am*, *are*, *aren't*, *is*, *isn't*, *was*, *wasn't*, *were*, and *weren't*. (There are others when you look at pronunciation details: *-'s* in *It's fine*; *-'m* in *I'm happy*; etc.)
- The lexeme *He* has only one shape in the pampering example, but there are others. Compare the underlined word-forms in <u>He</u> *likes pampering you, You should pamper* <u>him</u>, *It was* <u>his</u> *decision*, and *He should pamper* <u>himself</u>. They all have the same meaning, and can be collapsed together in one *He* lexeme in the dictionary.
- In the example sentence, *Like* is a regular verb lexeme with the word-forms *like*, *liked*, *liking*, and *likes*.
- *Pamper* is also a regular verb, with just the word-forms you'd predict by analogy: *pamper*, *pampered*, *pampering*, and *pampers*.
- *You* is a pronoun lexeme with the forms *you*, *your*, *yours*, and *yourself*.

In this book I'll classify lexemes into nine different major types which modern linguists call **categories**. (Traditional grammars use the rather strange term "parts of speech," which I will avoid. They're not parts of anything, and they have nothing specifically to do with speech; apart from that, it's a great name.)

- **Nouns** are a gigantic and constantly growing category containing tens of thousands of words, among which are the simplest ways of naming kinds of object (*Car, Lizard, Planet*, . . .) or substances (*Blood, Clay, Hydrogen*, . . .). The nouns include a very special subcategory called the **pronouns** (*They, We, Who*, . . .).

• **Verbs** constitute a very large category containing thousands of the most straightfoward ways of talking about voluntary or involuntary actions (*Announce, Educate, Shiver*, . . .) or relations (*Admire, Dislike, Precede*, . . .). There is a tiny but extremely important subcategory called the **auxiliary** verbs (the commonest ones are *Be, Can, Do, Have, May, Must, Ought, Shall*, and *Will*).

• **Adjectives** are a very large category of words often denoting permanent or temporary states or qualities (*Colorless, Intelligent, Obvious*, . . .). They are frequently used to modify meanings of nouns, and they include a medium-sized subcategory of **inflectable** adjectives: *Big* (with word-forms *bigger* and *biggest*), *Good* (with irregular word-forms *better* and *best*), *Polite* (with word-forms *politer* and *politest*), and so on.

• **Adverbs** are a very large category of words commonly used as modifiers (*Quite, Soon, Very*, . . .), of which the vast majority look like adjectives with *-ly* on the end (*Contentedly, Intelligently, Obviously*, . . .). They are frequently used to modify the sense of verbs, adjectives, prepositions, determinatives, and other adverbs.

• **Determinatives** are a very small category of generally short words that usually accompany nouns (*Most, Some, This*, . . .). They include the special case of the two **articles**, *An* (with word-forms *a* and *an*) and *The*.

• **Prepositions** are a medium-sized category of mostly short words (*At, By, In*, . . .). Many but not all make reference to relations in space (*Above, Beside, Under*, . . .) or relations in time (*After, Before, During*, . . .).

• **Subordinators** are an extremely small category of essentially meaningless words signaling the beginning of a clause

embedded inside another clause: the most important ones
are **That** (as in *I know that he lied*) and **Whether** (as in *I
wonder whether he lied*).

• **Coordinators** are a very small category of words for linking
clauses or phrases together with equal status; **And**, **Or**, and
Nor are examples.

• **Interjections** are a moderate-sized category of mostly short
words that interact very little with the grammar and often
simply signal the utterer's reactions (**Hey, Ouch, Wow**, . . .).

Categories are rather like what biological classification calls
"classes"; the mammals are an example. The species in a class
share important characteristics, but there can be decidedly
untypical members: the duck-billed platypus belongs in the
class of mammals, but has a beak and lays eggs; most members
of the class of birds fly, but penguins don't; and so on. For
a lexeme that is similarly unusual, take a look at **Beware**. It
belongs to the category of verbs, but it doesn't take any suffixes:
it has just one word-form. So we say *Beware of the dog*, or *You
should beware of the dog*, but we never find ~~He bewared of the
dog~~ or ~~I advise bewaring of the dog~~. It's best classified as a verb,
but it's a very strange one, a platypus among the verbs.

This means I will have to say "mostly" or "on the whole"
or "virtually all" many times in this book. It's not because I'm
being vague or haven't bothered to work things out in detail;
it's because of the nature of the phenomena. Human languages
are not neat and orderly and logical; the many complex and
subtle generalizations about them are (virtually always) riddled
with odd exceptions. And the reason is (as with odd hard-
to-classify animals) that it's simply what you should expect
when slow evolution proceeds over long timescales. It's been
hundreds of millions of years for animals, and only thousands
of years for languages, but in each case you have evolution
determined by partially random events and conditions.

4

Clause types

English has clauses of four grammatically distinct types, differing not just in their meanings, but also in their grammatical structure. The four types are: **declaratives**, **interrogatives**, **exclamatives**, and **imperatives**.

Subjects

Before we examine them, it will be useful to get clear on what a **subject** is. Traditional books define it as either "the doer of the action" or "what the sentence is about." Both definitions are useless. In *That seems reasonable*, the NP *that* is the subject, but there is no action and no "doer." And in *It will soon be winter*, the subject is *it*, but that doesn't tell us what is being talked about. The subject (of a clause, not a sentence) is an often obligatory NP of which the most interesting fact is that it often requires a verb to change its form: you have to say *Your parcel has arrived* (singular *parcel* so we need *has*), but *Your parcels have arrived* (plural *parcels* so the verb must be *have*). That is called **agreement** of the subject with the verb.

The four types

Now we can look at the four clause types. Grammarians tend to regard declaratives as the simplest and most basic, so we'll treat them first, and then look at interrogatives, exclamatives, and imperatives, each of which come in two variants. The summary list below exemplifies all four clause types:

CLAUSE TYPE	EXAMPLE	
declarative	*They were careful.*	
interrogative	*Were they careful?*	[closed]
	How careful were they?	[open]
exclamative	*How careful they were.*	[*how* type]
	What care they took!	[*what* type]
imperative	*Be careful!*	[no subject]
	You be careful!	[with subject]

Declarative clauses

Declarative clauses almost always have the subject BEFORE the verb, even an auxiliary verb: *They had been so careful.* (A minor exception is found when a negative modifier begins the clause in formal style: *Never had they been so careful* has the auxiliary before the subject pronoun.)

The TYPICAL use of declaratives is to express statements, but that's not their only use. The match between the clause types and the meanings they convey is quite flexible. A clause with declarative form can express a command (*You will go to your room right now*), or it can express a question, possibly even with a question mark at the end (*That was all you did?*).

Interrogative clauses

For **interrogative** clauses, expressing questions is the typical use. Questions are of two kinds: the ones with a fixed, closed set of acceptable answers and the ones with a wide-open set, and this is reflected in structure by the two kinds of interrogative main clause.

Closed interrogative main clauses express questions for which there is a closed and usually very short list of potential answers: *Do you come here often?* has only *Yes* and *No* as answers that would be appropriate and cooperative; *Would you like chicken, fish, or pasta?* has just three suitable answers. The key structural fact about closed interrogatives is that they always have an auxiliary verb before the subject: <u>*Will*</u> <u>*they*</u> *be careful?*

Open interrogative independent clauses are the ones that pose questions with a wide-open world of possible answers. An open interrogative begins with a special interrogative phrase containing *Who, What, Which, Where, When, Why*, or *How*, which I'll call *wh*-**words**. (*How* is spelled with its *w* at the end, but it behaves the same as the others.) If the interrogative phrase is the subject of the clause, it comes first, as subjects regularly do: <u>*How many users*</u> <u>*will*</u> *be that careful?* But if the interrogative phrase is not the subject, an auxiliary verb comes next, BEFORE the subject: *How careful <u>will</u> <u>they</u> be?*

The TV quiz game *Jeopardy!* provides a nice illustration of why the form of a clause mustn't be confused with the sort of meaning it usually expresses. Contestants are supposed to give their answers in interrogative form, so if the quizmaster says, "He was president but resigned in 1974," the right response would be something like "Who was Richard Nixon?" But the contestant isn't posing a question or seeking an answer; the interrogative clause that a successful contestant offers is an **answer**, not a question!

Exclamative clauses

Exclamative clauses always begin with either *how* or *what*, but they differ crucially from open interrogatives in having the subject before any auxiliary verb. That's the only difference in structure between *How careful they were!* (exclamative) and *How careful were they?* (interrogative).

Exclamatives are characteristically used to express surprise or elation at the degree of something, like the extent of the remarkable care they took, but it's important that an exclamation of that sort doesn't have to be expressed with an exclamative. (Many grammar books are hopelessly confused on that point, and think anything exciting or anything ending in "!" is an exclamative. Not true!)

Everyone hears exclamatives. For example, they occur in lots of song titles (*What a difference a day makes*; *What a fool I am*; *How sweet it is*; *What a friend we have in Jesus*; *How great Thou art*). And there's a celebrated line in the film of *Harry Potter and the Half-Blood Prince* where Severus Snape tells Harry coldly: *How grand it must be, to be the Chosen One.*

But the exclamative clause type is definitely less frequent than it used to be. It often sounds somewhat old-fashioned or literary. Younger speakers tend to replace exclamatives by clauses with interrogative form. They'll say *Did we have a blast!* (interrogative form, but not a question!) instead of *What a blast we had!* (exclamative), or *How cool is that!* (interrogative form) rather than *How cool that is!* (exclamative).

Imperative clauses

Imperative clauses such as *Be careful!* have several very special properties. First, if we set aside casual speech (*Mustn't be late*), the imperative is the only type of main clause that can lack a subject NP before the verb. Second, it's the only clause type that can't be embedded as a complement in a larger clause. And third, setting aside a few grammatical fossils like *Be that as it may* or *God be praised* that are inherited from earlier centuries, the imperative is the only common type of main clause that has its main verb in the PLAIN FORM.

When an imperative does have a subject, it has to be something that can refer to the addressee. It's often *you* (as in *You take care, now!*), but it can be some other phrase that allows the sentence to be understood as a directive to everyone addressed, as in *All rise* (to get everyone in a courtroom to stand), or *Everybody calm down!* (addressed to a rowdy meeting), or *Nobody move!* (to make sure nobody in the bank does anything stupid).

The typical use of imperatives (though not their only use) is to get people to do things: ordering, instructing, or advising them. This doesn't have to be bossy: *Sleep well* simply gives encouraging good wishes for a restful night; *Help yourself to some coffee* gives permission rather than telling someone what to do. So don't make the mistake of confusing **imperatives** (which are clauses of a specific form) with **commands** (which are actions people take).

Notice too that in *Get it wrong and they'll fail you*, the clause *get it wrong* has imperative form (with no subject), but when joined with *and* to a declarative like this, it's not understood as a directive: the sentence means "If you get it wrong, they'll fail you."

5

Nouns and their phrases

Every language on earth has a huge fund of words of a special type that linguists call **nouns**. In a language like English, with hundreds of millions of speakers living in complex modern societies where a lot of invention goes on, new nouns are coined just about every day, as we invent names for new artifacts (*blockchain*), create new model or product names (*Elantra*), and adopt useful terms from other languages (*wasabi*).

In the paragraph above there were twenty different noun lexemes (some used more than once), not counting the three example words in italics. Here they are again in alphabetical order:

Artifact	*Day*	*Earth*	*English*
Fund	*Hundred*	*Invention*	*Language*
Linguist	*Lot*	*Million*	*Model*
Name	*Noun*	*Product*	*Society*
Speaker	*Term*	*Type*	*Word*

Traditional grammars of the past three hundred years define nouns as "naming words"; often they are said to be names for "persons, places, or things." But that's hopeless as a definition. It suggests that the way to decide which words are nouns would be by first looking around to see what things exist, and then locating the words that name them. But just consider the nouns listed above. Look around you. How are you going to determine that the world contains days, hundreds, inventions, languages, lots, millions, names, nouns, products, societies, terms, or types? These notions are far too abstract for that to be possible; they refer to invisible processes, categories, quantities, periods, units, or concepts. With some it isn't clear whether they refer to anything at all: consider *I like her a whole lot* or *Do this for my sake*, and ask yourself whether the nouns *lot* or *sake* name things.

The more you reflect on this issue the worse the traditional view looks. Step outside with a notebook and make notes on whether you can spot any abandonments, aberrations, absences, acquittals, acres, admissions, affections, ailments, alibis, allowances, anachronisms, annoyances, arousals, arrangements, attributions, awakenings, azimuths. . . These are not things in any normal sense!

A sensible way to explain what a noun is would run like this. The category of nouns is a distinctive set of words which includes all the simple one-word names for types of ordinary physical objects like apples, and one-word names for types of stuff such as gold, but in addition includes all the thousands of other words that behave similarly in grammatical terms – that is, they fit into sentences in just the same sorts of places.

Count nouns

The lexemes that really do name kinds of countable things are the only ones for which the traditional definition works. These are called **count nouns**. They include *Apple, Box, Cat, Dog, Elephant, Fork, Gun, House, Idiot, Jar, Key, Lamp, Monkey,*

Nail, Orange, Pear, Queen, Rabbit, Sock, Table, Umbrella,
Vase, Worm, Xylophone, Yacht, Zebra, and thousands of
others. Notice, they don't actually name particular things;
they name kinds of things. My dining room table doesn't have
a name. The lexeme *Table* is a name for that sort of object,
and it's as applicable to your dining room table as it is to mine.
(We'll come to the special nouns that do name individual
things in a minute.)

Count nouns in English (but not in all languages) virtually
always have separate **singular** forms (as in the list above) and
plural forms, mostly formed by putting *s* (or *es*) on the end
of the singular (*apples, boxes, cats,* etc.). A few have irregular
plurals. Some have minor changes like an *f* in the singular
becoming *v* in the plural (*knife, knives; life, lives; wife, wives*).
The familiar singular nouns *man, woman,* and *child* have
totally unpredictable plurals (*men, women, children*). In a few
cases nouns borrowed from Latin or Greek keep their original
plurals, and don't follow any native English pattern:

SINGULAR	PLURAL	SINGULAR	PLURAL
addendum	*addenda*	*index*	*indices*
alumnus	*alumni*	*labium*	*labia*
analysis	*analyses*	*larva*	*larvae*
antithesis	*antitheses*	*locus*	*loci*
automaton	*automata*	*matrix*	*matrices*
axis	*axes*	*medium*	*media*
bacterium	*bacteria*	*metamorphosis*	*metamorphoses*
basis	*bases*	*neurosis*	*neuroses*
cactus	*cacti*	*nucleus*	*nuclei*
codex	*codices*	*oasis*	*oases*
corpus	*corpora*	*opus*	*opera*
corrigendum	*corrigenda*	*parenthesis*	*parentheses*
cortex	*cortices*	*phenomenon*	*phenomena*
crisis	*crises*	*phylum*	*phyla*
criterion	*criteria*	*prolegomenon*	*prolegomena*
curriculum	*curricula*	*psychosis*	*psychoses*
datum	*data*	*quantum*	*quanta*

SINGULAR	PLURAL	SINGULAR	PLURAL
desideratum	desiderata	radius	radii
diagnosis	diagnoses	stimulus	stimuli
ellipsis	ellipses	stratum	strata
emphasis	emphases	syllabus	syllabi
erratum	errata	synopsis	synopses
fungus	fungi	synthesis	syntheses
ganglion	ganglia	terminus	termini
genus	genera	thesis	theses
hippopotamus	hippopotami	thrombosis	thromboses
hypothesis	hypotheses	vortex	vortices

Even though most of these have plurals defined by Latin or Greek grammar, and it's not fair to expect you to know Latin or Greek, you are expected to know the plurals listed above if you want to be regarded as literate in English. **Phenomenon** may not be a particularly frequent word, but it's common enough to make it very important to remember that *phenomenon* is the singular and *phenomena* the plural. People wrongly use details of this sort as if they were signs of intelligence level, so it's worth memorizing the right plurals.

Mass nouns

There are other nouns that refer not to countable items but to types of stuff, which means it's unusual for them to be used in the plural: *Air, Beef, Coffee, Dust, Earth, Foam, Garlic, Honey, Ice, Jelly, Kelp, Lava, Milk, Nectar, Oil, Pork, Quartz, Rhubarb, Smoke, Tar, Urine, Venom, Water, Xenon, Yogurt, Zinc*, and so on.

The twenty-six mass nouns I just listed were picked because you hardly ever hear them in the plural, but huge numbers of mass nouns have a second use in which they behave like count nouns and refer to either conventional units of the stuff or different varieties of the stuff. Those uses do have a plural form: *coffees* means either cups of coffee or varieties of coffee; *oils* might be used for types of oil or for oil paintings; *foams* could mean kinds of foam; and so on. But for lexemes like **Gold** or **Zinc** you'll probably never encounter a plural form because there are neither familiar associated units nor significantly different varieties of those substances.

A small minority of nouns that refer to materials or collections of objects pretty much NEVER show up in the plural: **Clothing**, **Crockery**, **Equipment**, **Furniture**, **Wreckage**, and a small number of others. There are also a tiny number of peculiar nouns found ONLY in the plural: **Auspices**, **Clothes**, **Dribs**, **Pants**, **Scissors**, **Throes**, and a few other words relating to things we speak of as if they necessarily come in pairs or groups.

Just to make things even more like biology, with its strange exceptional animals, some nouns seem to be neither mass nor count. Compare *Mist* with *Midst*, for example. They have to be nouns: *in the midst of the turmoil* is just like *in the heart of the city* or *in the mist of the morning*. The phrase *more mist* is grammatical, and so is *several mists*, so **Mist** is both a mass noun and a count noun. But now consider ~~more midst~~ and ~~several midsts~~. Both are impossible, so **Midst** seems to be neither mass nor count. (Never underestimate the strange little quirks of the grammar of English; it's a linguistic jungle out there.)

Abstract nouns

The most obvious reason that we can't call nouns "thing words" is that thousands of abstract notions, not like things or stuff in any normal sense, are named by nouns. Some of these nouns (like **Absence**, **Appeal**, **Failure**, **Intricacy**, **Protection**, **Similarity**, **Year**) are count nouns, so they have plurals:

SINGULAR	PLURAL
absence	*absences*
appeal	*appeals*
failure	*failures*
intricacy	*intricacies*
protection ˙	*protections*
similarity	*similarities*
year	*years*

Other abstract concepts are named by mass nouns, so they don't have plurals (or at least, their plurals are virtually never encountered): **Abolition, Boredom, Cautiousness, Decadence, Enmity, Faith,** and so on. But it would be deeply weird to say that the word *absence* names a kind of thing, or that the word *decadence* names a kind of stuff.

Proper nouns

All the count nouns, mass nouns, and abstract nouns we've just looked at are known as **common nouns**. They can often be used with *the* and/or *a(n)*, which are called the **articles**. But there is also a huge special subcategory of nouns that almost never occur with articles, and are hardly ever seen in the plural. They're the ones known as the **proper** nouns. ("Proper" here doesn't mean "appropriate" or "well-mannered"; it's an older use meaning "referring or belonging to just a single individual.") Proper nouns provide names for individual people, places, companies, days, or other unique entities. They're always singular and almost always spelled with a capital initial letter: **Africa, Borneo, Christmas, Denmark, Everest, France, Georgia, Hamburg, Ireland, Jamaica, Kelvin, Libya, Microsoft, Neptune, Oakland, Paris, Qatar, Ritz, Swahili, Turing, Uruguay, Virginia, Watergate, Xerxes, Yellowstone, Zimbabwe,** and so on.

Proper nouns normally don't occur with articles (~~the Africa~~) or in the plural (~~Africas~~), but they can when their meaning shifts a bit: you can call someone *a second Turing* to mean another genius computer theorist, or *several Christmases* to mean several years' occurrences of December 25. But these are exceptions to the normal use.

A very small number of other words (not noticed by any previous grammar as far as I know) behave just like proper nouns but don't invariably take a capital initial letter. The lexemes **Today**, **Yesterday**, and **Tomorrow** denote specific days (the one you're in, the one before, and the one after). There are also a small number of words for specific non-physical places or states of being, like **Heaven**, **Hell**, **Limbo**, **Nirvana**, **Paradise**, **Purgatory**, and perhaps a few others. **Earth** tends not to be capitalized in phrases like *nowhere else on earth*, but capitalized when we're mentioning it along with other planets: *from Mars to Earth*. These words all usually occur in the singular and without articles, so the best view would be that they're proper nouns, whether capitalized or not.

Notice that there's a reason I write lexeme names with capital letters: each one is really a proper noun denoting a specific word in the dictionary.

Noun phrases

Phrases are groups of words, organized around a principal word known as the **head**, working together as a unit to form an identifiable component of a sentence. A noun is almost always the principal word in a **Noun Phrase**. (I'll note one or two minor exceptions later.) This term will turn up often, and I'll always abbreviate it as **NP**. Various additional words such as articles and adjectives may occur in an NP. The head noun in each of these examples is *Car*:

my car
the car of my dreams
the luxury car that the two of them arrived in
several expensive foreign cars
the thousands of cars in the airport parking structure
several brand new cars on the deck of a massive container ship

The first three have singular head nouns, so they're singular NPs. The last three are **plural** NPs, because of their plural head noun.

When a proper noun like *London* or a plural common noun like *birds* occurs with no other words in its phrase, I'll still count it as a one-word phrase. That may seem a bit strange at first (like a club with only one member?), but it's very helpful: if you don't allow one-word NPs, you have to repeatedly say "either a noun or an NP" throughout any grammatical description.

Proper names

It's very important to distinguish **proper nouns** like *Washington* from **proper names** like *the White House*. Traditional grammars often don't. Proper names are NPs referring to specific people, places, institutions, or other entities; they often contain proper nouns, but often don't (there is no proper noun in *the White House*, despite the capital letters), and they may contain other words as well, like *the* or *of,* or common nouns, or adjectives. They can be singular or plural. In some proper names the word *the* is obligatory (but notice, *the* doesn't have a capital letter, unless it's at the beginning of a sentence!): *the Pentagon, the Kennedy Center, the Atlantic Ocean, the Sahara Desert, the Virgin Islands, the Great Lakes, the Rocky Mountains,* and so on.

Not all proper names begin with *the*: there are thousands of proper names like *Buckingham Palace, Carnegie Hall, Edinburgh Castle, Lake Superior, Lincoln Center, Los Angeles International Airport, Wild Turkey, Madison Square Gardens, Western Sahara.*

Plain and genitive NPs

NPs have a **genitive** form with certain special uses as well as an ordinary or **plain** form. It is marked by *'s* added to the end of the last word of the NP – or just the apostrophe (*'*) when the last word is a head noun in the regular plural form. In these examples the largest genitive NP is shown in a box (notice that there can be a genitive NP inside another genitive NP):

the commander in chief's *decision*
the sergeant major's *voice*
the Duke of Edinburgh's *car*
the person I spoke to's *attitude*
all of my friends' *bicycles*
the Beatles' *first album*
successive governments' *lamentable failures*
Santa's elves' *ugly green costumes*

Because of genitive marking, a typical NP in written English will have four different spellings (though three of them have exactly the same pronunciation). Most often (but not always) it's the head noun itself that determines the spelling. Here are the four shapes for a typical regular noun:

	SINGULAR	PLURAL
PLAIN	*box*	*boxes*
GENITIVE	*box's*	*boxes'*

With regular nouns like *box*, all the word-forms except for the plain singular (i.e., the plain plural *boxes*, the genitive singular *box's*, and the genitive plural *boxes'*) sound exactly the same when pronounced (try saying them out loud), but they're spelled differently. With an irregular noun like *man*, *woman*, or *child*, however, they all sound different as well as being spelled differently:

	SINGULAR	PLURAL
PLAIN	*man, woman, child*	*men, women, children*
GENITIVE	*man's, woman's, child's*	*men's, women's, children's*

Apostrophes are used to form **genitives**, not **plurals**. The nitpickers of the grammar world are strongly allergic to seeing people use -'s for a plural (or leave it out in a genitive). When they see a supermarket advertising ~~fresh tomato's~~, they write letters to newspapers about how horrified they were. So (forgive me for shouting this) NEVER USE AN APOSTROPHE TO FORM A PLURAL. (For a very limited exception to that, see page 147.)

Pronouns

One very small but especially important subset of the nouns is called the **pronouns**. These are short words that behave as full NPs. Traditional grammars treat them separately from nouns, often in a different chapter, and give them a definition saying that a pronoun is a word used to make reference to people or things as a substitute for a full name or description. But separating them from the nouns is a mistake. So is the definition, which I'll come back to shortly.

Pronouns are much more like proper nouns than like anything else. They hardly ever occur with determinatives or adjectives. The most important grammatical difference between pronouns and other nouns is that they show an extra classificatory distinction known as **person**: they are classified according to the person or thing referred to. We use the terms **1st, 2nd,** or **3rd** in the following way:

• The two pronouns of the **1st-person** type are *I*, which refers just to the utterer, and *We*, which usually refers to a group including the utterer. (There are a few minor and unimportant exceptions to that: doctors saying things like *How are we feeling today, Mrs. Glenmont?*; monarchs in earlier times referring to themselves with the royal *We*; and scientists who follow the strange practice of always pretending to be a team: *We supply fuller details in our PhD dissertation.*)

- There are two **2nd-person** pronoun lexemes which never make reference to the utterer, referring either to just the addressee or to the addressee and at least one other person. They share most of their forms; I'll call them *You*$_{sg}$ and *You*$_{pl}$. You can see they have different forms in *You embarrassed yourself* vs. *You all embarrassed yourselves*.

- **3rd-person** pronouns refer neither to the utterer nor to the addressee. (The same is typically true for all the ordinary NPs that aren't pronouns, so they are 3rd person as well.) *He*, *It*, and *She* are singular 3rd-person pronouns, and so is the curious item I'll call *One*$_{pro}$ that we see in *One must look after oneself.* There are also two pronouns sharing the shape *they*: a plural one I'll call *They*$_{pl}$, and a singular one I'll call *They*$_{sg}$. (The long but mistaken tradition of calling *They*$_{sg}$ a grammatical error is briefly discussed later, in chapter 16.)

The different 3rd-person pronouns in English have meanings that presuppose different things about the nature of the entity or entities they are used to refer to:

- *He* implies that the entity referred to is a boy or man, or perhaps an identifiably male animal or something that we personify that way (male dogs; masculine-looking robots). There is an extraordinary but widespread belief abroad that *He* can be used as a gender-neutral pronoun, as if *any engineer who knows his job* could cover female engineers. Though originally promoted by a woman (Ann Fisher, an English grammarian who published a number of works between 1745 and 1778), the idea has no basis in the facts of

English. Think about why it would sound so utterly crazy to say *?Did one of your parents injure himself?*, or *?If your brother or your sister wants to come, we can invite him.* The reason is that *He* is never neutral about sex: it always implies reference to a boy or man. This didn't keep Winston Churchill from actually saying in a 1940 speech, as the German campaign of bombing London began, that "Every man and woman will therefore prepare himself to do his duty." He stuck rigidly to the spurious rule that Ann Fisher had invented. But I think it's clear that it sounds hilariously inappropriate today.

• *She* is used for girls or women, and anything else that we personify as classified with them (feminine-looking robots, and sometimes ships, cars, or countries in older literature). For that reason, *She* does no better than *He* as a candidate for referring to a third party without implying anything about sex: *The reader can find out for herself* implies that the reader is female.

• *It* is used for referring to inanimate objects or animals not readily identified as male or female. That sometimes includes very young humans (*The baby was asleep and we tried not to wake it*), but that's much less common than it used to be.

• *One*$_{pro}$ is used solely in formal style, to refer to any arbitrary human, as in *One should never perjure oneself*. Sometimes it will tacitly be a bashful reference to the utterer (*One does what one can to help the poor*). The alternative in informal style is to use the singular 2nd-person pronoun *You*$_{sg}$ (unstressed, so it sounds more like *ya* or *yuh*, and is sometimes written that way): *You try not to show your feelings or embarrass yourself* would be the informal version of *One tries not to show one's feelings or embarrass oneself.*

• *They*$_{pl}$ doesn't presuppose anything about the people or things referred to other than that there's more than one of them.

- ***They***$_{sg}$ is different in that respect: it presupposes reference to a human, but without specifying gender. So we get *Someone reported that <u>they</u> left <u>their</u> umbrella in the restaurant*, but not ~~*This dog has lost their owner*~~ or ~~*That parcel has lost their label*~~.

Reflexive pronoun forms

Pronoun lexemes also have a **reflexive** form ending in *-self* (or *-selves*), used to refer to the same person or entity as some NP earlier in the same clause: <u>*She*</u> *was so pleased with* <u>*herself*</u>; <u>*They*</u> *surprised* <u>*themselves*</u>. Sometimes in modern usage ***They***$_{sg}$ has the reflexive form *themself*, as in *Sometimes a person can surprise themself.* (Microsoft Word's grammar-checking tool doesn't like this, and peremptorily changes it to *themselves* – what a nerve!)

Plural pronoun forms

The singular/plural distinction doesn't apply to pronouns in anything like the same way as with ordinary nouns, but it's standard practice to use the terms "singular" and "plural" for them anyway, and I'll follow the tradition: we'll use the terms "singular" and "plural" to distinguish *I* from *We* (despite the fact that *We* certainly doesn't refer to a collection of people each one of whom is me!), and *It* from ***They***$_{pl}$, and *You*$_{sg}$ from *You*$_{pl}$.

Two kinds of genitive

All nouns have a genitive form, but pronouns have two of them. The **dependent genitive** form is used before a head noun, and the **independent genitive** form (usually distinct) is used on its own but with a genitive-related meaning. To illustrate with *I*: we get _my painting_, where *my* is the dependent genitive of *I*, but *That painting is _mine_*, where *mine* is the independent genitive and effectively means "my painting."

Nominative and accusative

There is one other special distinction that pronouns have but other nouns don't: some pronouns have two different special non-genitive forms instead of a single plain form. I'll illustrate with the pronoun *I* again:

- The **nominative** form *I* is used when the pronoun is a subject, as in _I agree_. Some very conservative older books suggest that you should use it after the verb *Be*, but I don't recommend it, because it sounds unbearably pompous. If your friend calls out, "Who's there?" when you knock on her door and you say, "It is I," she probably won't even let you in. If it were normal in English to use the nominative after *Be*, then this should sound just fine:

    ~~Let's switch roles: I can be you and you can be I.~~

    But no normal person would talk or write like that. They would say *I can be you and you can be me*. Something similar is true about *Be* following *than*: *?No one would be happier than I* is recommended in older books, but it makes you sound like a 90-year-old English aristocrat, which might not be the image you have of yourself. A normal person would say *No one would be happier than me*.
- The **accusative** form is used for non-genitive pronouns that aren't subjects: *Watch _me_* has the accusative form of *I*. It is also used when the rest of the sentence doesn't provide a

context that makes the pronoun a subject, as in one-word answers to questions. A hungry person's answer to "Who wants some pizza?" will typically be "*Me!*"

The full set of pronoun forms

So the full picture of the forms for English pronouns is shown in the following tables (and you'll see that I've put arrows where in five instances there's a form spelled exactly like the one in the box above it – that's yet another case of irregularity). The irregularities here are much like the other irregularities in English inflections. *It*, *You*$_{sg}$, and *You*$_{pl}$ don't distinguish the nominative from the accusative (the up arrows mean "use the form above"); *She* has a dependent genitive that happens to be the same shape as its accusative; and *He* and *It* don't show any difference between dependent and independent genitive forms.

SINGULAR PRONOUNS

	1ST PERSON	2ND PERSON	3RD PERSON			
			MASC.	FEM.	COMMON	NEUT.
NOMINATIVE	*I*	*you*	*he*	*she*	*they*	*it*
ACCUSATIVE	*me*	↑	*him*	*her*	*them*	↑
DEPENDENT GENITIVE	*my*	*your*	*his*	↑	*their*	*its*
INDEPENDENT GENITIVE	*mine*	*yours*	↑	*hers*	*theirs*	↑
REFLEXIVE	*myself*	*yourself*	*himself*	*herself*	*themself*	*itself*

PLURAL PRONOUNS

	1ST PERSON	2ND PERSON	3RD PERSON
NOMINATIVE	we	you	they
ACCUSATIVE	us	↑	them
DEPENDENT GENITIVE	our	your	their
INDEPENDENT GENITIVE	ours	yours	theirs
REFLEXIVE	ourselves	yourselves	themselves

What pronouns do

Traditional grammars define pronouns as words that stand in place of nouns. (It would have been a bit closer to the mark to say they stand in place of NPs.) You can see what this is getting at in sentences like:

> *Montmorency thought he could get away with awarding himself a prize for his work.*

The pronouns *he* and *himself* allow the speaker to avoid three repetitions of Montmorency's four-syllable name. But this use can't be used as the basis for a definition of pronouns, because there is often no NP that you could reasonably say had been replaced. Take a sentence like this (where I underline the pronouns):

> *It really impressed me the way you politely made it clear that we disagreed.*

Not one of the five pronouns in this sentence could be said to be standing in for other NPs we could have used instead. The first *it* doesn't refer to anything or stand in place of anything; *me* refers directly to whoever is speaking, regardless of their name or description; *you* refers directly to the person addressed (and the utterer might not know the addressee's name); the second *it* is again meaningless and couldn't be replaced by any other NP; and *we* refers directly to some group of people including the speaker but is ambiguous about whether it includes the addressee, so we wouldn't know which list of NPs to use.

Defining pronouns

There are, however, properties that can be used to give a more accurate definition of the pronoun category. I'll mention just two. First, like proper nouns, they never normally take articles or modifying adjectives. (In the very rare exceptions to this, like *This isn't <u>the you</u> I fell in love with*, the pronoun has a different meaning – in this example, *the you* means something like "the version of you" or "the person that you formerly were.")

Second, a useful test is provided by the mini-questions called **confirmation tags** that people sometimes add to sentences in conversation to ask for confirmation of agreement, like the underlined parts of these sentences:

> *That was unprecedented, <u>wasn't it</u>?*
> *She's really smart, <u>isn't she</u>?*
> *One does what one can, <u>doesn't one</u>?*
> *We weren't really ready for that one, <u>were we</u>?*

The first part of a tag is always an **auxiliary verb** (a negative one if the earlier part of the clause was positive, or a positive one if the earlier part of the clause was negative), and the second part is always a pronoun. Even short names that rhyme with pronouns can't appear in tags:

> *Dee's a genius, <u>isn't she</u>?*   *Dee's a genius, <u>isn't Dee</u>?*
> *You will be there, <u>won't you</u>?*   *Hugh will be there, <u>won't Hugh</u>?*
> *I looked pretty silly, <u>didn't I</u>?*   *Guy looked pretty silly, <u>didn't Guy</u>?*

So for a working definition we could say that the pronouns are a small fixed class of very special short nouns that hardly ever take articles or modifying adjectives but are permitted as the NPs in confirmation tags.

6

Determinatives

Now it's time to get more serious about the articles and similar words. The **determinatives** are a small class of lexemes including the two **articles** already mentioned (the **indefinite** article *An* and the **definite** article *The*), plus *This* and *That*$_\text{det}$ (often called **demonstratives**), and thirty or forty other words (many referring to quantities or extents) such as *All, Any, Both, Each, Either, Every, Few, Many, No, Several*, and *Some*. All of the numeral words (*one, two, three, four*, . . .) also belong among the determinatives, so in that sense the category is gigantic.

I should mention in passing that many books use "determiner" for the category of words that I call determinatives. But using my terminology, the words "adjective," "demonstrative," and "determinative" all end in *-ive* and are all names of categories (classes of words). The right use for the word **determiner**, I think, is as a name for what determinatives usually do: they serve a special purpose in NPs that can also be served by genitive NPs. In both <u>*the dean's*</u> *list* and <u>*that*</u> *list*, the underlined word is a **determiner** of the head noun *list*. The words "modifier" and "determiner" both end in *-er*, and they're both **functions**. They name roles that constituents can play, not categories or types of constituent. This may be a tricky point of terminology, but trust me, it's better to use terms this way than to get confused about what's a category and what's a function.

The determinative *An* has the word-form *a* when it comes immediately before a consonant sound, like the sounds normally spelled with letters like *b, c, d, f, g, j, k, l, m, n, p, r, s, t, w, z*. It has the form *an* immediately before a vowel sound. Notice, it's SOUNDS we're talking about, not letters, so the chaos of English spelling can be grossly misleading. We get *a horrible act, a usually friendly dog, a ewe, a hotel, a unicorn, a yellow sign*; but we get *an honorable act, an unusually friendly dog, an emu, an honest man, an unknown animal, an ytterbium laser*. (Say these out loud and this will all begin to make sense.)

The determinative *This* has the word-form *this* when it's the determiner of a singular NP, and *these* when it's the determiner in a plural one. *That*$_{det}$ (where "det" is a reminder that this is the demonstrative determinative, not the different word that appears in *I know that you're lying*) has the singular form *that* and the plural form *those*.

Determinatives going it alone

With just three exceptions, all of the determinatives can stand alone as NPs, like this:

> *<u>All</u> were saved.*
> *<u>Some</u> like it hot.*
> *<u>Most</u> were rejected.*
> *You can have <u>either</u>, or <u>both</u>.*
> *We found a few clues, but <u>none</u> were helpful.*

Typically, an NP has a head, but determinatives other than *An*, *Every*, and *The* (those are the three exceptions) are allowed to stand on their own as if they were head nouns. So a determinative can serve as the only word in an NP.

A phrase with *of* and an NP (it's called a "**partitive** PP") can be popped in after the determinative to indicate the class of things from which the specified set is drawn:

> All *of the children* were saved.
> Some *of us* like it hot.
> Most *of the applicants* were rejected.
> You can have either *of the desserts,* or both [= "both of the desserts"]
> We found a few clues, but none *of the clues that we found* were useful.

A singular count noun can combine with *one, a(n), the, every, this, that,* or any other singular-compatible determinative to make a singular NP. A plural noun can serve as an NP on its own, or with any other plural-compatible determinative (such as *the, these, those, many, most, few,* or any numeral other than *one*) to make a plural NP.

SINGULAR	PLURAL
this apple	*these apples*
one box	*two boxes*
every house	*all houses*
that potato	*those potatoes*
any table	*any tables*
this zebra	*most zebras*

Pre-determiner *All* and *Both*

You generally only get one determinative per NP, so examples like ~~the both children~~ or ~~a this clever trick~~ or ~~some most cookies~~ are impossible. But just two special determinatives, *All* and *Both,* can occur before the determinative of an NP as **pre-determiners**:

> *All the* chairs were damaged.
> I love *both my* children.

These are expressible in an alternative way, which follows from what I said above:

All [*of the chairs*] *were damaged.*
I love both [*of my children*].

Here *all* and *both* are being used the way they are in *All were damaged* or *I love both*, but partitive PPs have been added. But that doesn't mean you can just say that the *of* in partitive PPs can be left out, because that isn't true. It would give you all sorts of wrong results. You can't leave out the *of* in *those of the children who were eligible* to get ~~those the children who were eligible~~. The pre-determiner use is a special feature of *All* and **Both**, not the result of dropping an *of*. (Beware simplistic guesses at what the rules are. The rule here is not "*Of* can be omitted"!)

7

Verbs

The verbs form a very large class of lexemes – thousands and thousands of them. They include all the simplest single-word ways of naming actions, or things a person could do: *Assess, Betray, Caress, Decide, Eliminate, Forge, Give, Hinder, Investigate, Jostle, Keep, Linger, Memorize, Nibble, Obtain, Pierce, Quit, Ravage, Succeed, Tremble, Understand, Vanish, Weep, X-ray, Yawn, Zoom,* and so on.

Because of examples like ones in the list above, verbs are often referred to as "doing words." But verbs don't always name actions. Huge numbers of them refer to being in certain states, not to actions in any ordinary sense, yet they have all the same sort of syntactic behavior as the verbs listed above. For example, in a sentence like *It seems hot in here*, the verb *seems* couldn't possibly be said to identify an action. Much the same is true for verbs like *Abhor, Be, Contain, Decrease, Exceed, Forget, Glisten, Have, Impend, Justify, Keep, Languish, Merit, Necrotize, Outrank,* . . . Think about the meanings of these verbs: they are difficult or impossible to conceptualize as actions.

Nearly all verbs have a basic form that I'll call the **plain form**, used in various contexts. It will be convenient to use the plain form of a verb as the lexeme name. The plain forms of the verbs listed in the preceding paragraph are *abhor, be, contain, decrease,* and so on. But verbs have various other forms, mostly formed by adding suffixes on the end of the plain form. **Abhor**, for example, has *abhors, abhorred,* and *abhorring.* To explain what these differing forms of verbs are for, we first need the concept of tense.

Tense

Almost all verbs show a contrast in **tense**, which is mostly employed to show how an event or state is located in time. The **present** tense is used to situate events or states in the current moment (*I recommend it*) or to talk about things that are timeless (*People always say that*). The **past** tense form, which in regular verbs has an *ed* added to the plain form, is used to locate events or states in past time (*I recommended it*).

The term "past tense" encourages you to think it's referring to past time, but that isn't always true. The past tense form sometimes refers to the situation in an unreal hypothetical world different from the real one: the sentence *If I investigated further, would I find out anything bad?* is not about a past investigation that I undertook; it's about an imaginary one that I conceivably might undertake in the future. And sometimes a past tense just seems to be trying to put things more diffidently or politely: *I wondered if I could possibly borrow your car* isn't necessarily about what I wondered in the past, it can be about what I'm wondering right now.

Now that I've introduced tense, I can improve the precision of something I said earlier, about how the nominative form is used when a pronoun is the subject. To be more careful, we should say that the nominative occurs when the pronoun is the subject IN A CLAUSE WHERE THE VERB HAS PAST OR PRESENT TENSE FORM, or, for short, in a **tensed clause**).

Past participles

Nearly all verbs also have a form traditionally known as the **past participle**. (That's not a great name, because it really doesn't have much to do with the past, but it's standard, and I'll use it.) Although the past participle has completely different uses from the past tense, regular verbs have past participles that look and sound exactly the same as their past tense. So *Yesterday we assessed the damage* illustrates the past tense of **Assess**; *We have now assessed the damage* illustrates the past participle (and notice, it speaks about the present).

Irregular verbs

Nearly two hundred verbs in English have **irregular** past tense forms. Some change a vowel letter in the middle (*run, ran*); some use a *t* on the end instead of a *d* (*send, sent*); some change a vowel and add a *t* (*keep, kept*); some change nothing (*They always let me out on weekends* is present, *They let me out last weekend* is past); and one or two verbs change the whole word-shape (the weird past tense form of **Go** is *went*, and for *is* we get the past tense *was*).

There are also many irregular verbs whose past participles aren't the same shape as the past tense. If you have spoken English since you were a toddler, you've already had a wonderful stroke of luck, because many of the irregular verbs are extremely common, and you will have learned nearly all of them unconsciously without even realizing how strange they are. Here are ten examples of irregular verbs that happen to have past participles identical to their past tense forms:

PRESENT TENSE	PAST TENSE / PAST PARTICIPLE
feel	*felt*
find	*found*
have	*had*
leave	*left*
make	*made*
sell	*sold*
send	*sent*
stand	*stood*
think	*thought*
win	*won*

And here are ten other even more irregular verbs, in which the past participle happens to be different from the past tense:

PRESENT TENSE	PAST TENSE	PAST PARTICIPLE
choose	*chose*	*chosen*
come	*came*	*come*
drive	*drove*	*driven*
fall	*fell*	*fallen*
give	*gave*	*given*
go	*went*	*gone*
hide	*hid*	*hidden*
see	*saw*	*seen*
sing	*sang*	*sung*
take	*took*	*taken*

Gerund-participles

There is one other form that nearly every verb has. I'll call it the **gerund-participle**. It is formed in a totally regular way: every verb that has a gerund-participle forms it by simply adding *ing* to the end of the plain form of the verb (dropping a silent *e* if there is one in the spelling). So for *be* we get *being*, for *come* we get *coming*, for *go* we get *going*, for *have* we get *having*, and so on. There's no problem about the shapes.

Auxiliary verbs

Although most English verbs belong to a huge class that I will call the **lexical** verbs, there is a crucially important very small subclass of verbs known as the **auxiliary** verbs. (This traditional name implies that all they do is help other verbs out, and traditionally they are often called "helping verbs." That's a bad name and a bad definition, because sometimes these verbs don't occur with any other verb they could help. But the term "auxiliary" is very well established, so I'll use it.) In most varieties of English (with a very small amount of variation, especially between American and British) we find only about a dozen auxiliary verb lexemes.

The three most basic ones are *Be*, as in *You should be dancing*, *Do*, as in *Do you come here often?*, and *Have*, as in *You have lost your mind*. (The last two have uses as lexical verbs, so we may need to name the auxiliaries Do_{aux} and $Have_{aux}$.)

The auxiliary verbs are identified not by their meaning but by several crucial grammatical properties:

- Auxiliary verbs have **negative** forms with the suffix *-n't* for most of their present and past tense forms, so there are pairs like *do/don't*, *does/doesn't*, *have/haven't*, *has/hasn't*, *is/isn't*, *was/wasn't*. Lexical verbs never have *-n't* forms. Traditional grammars call these *n't* forms "contractions," as if *don't* was just the result of saying *do not* so swiftly that the two words merge. But that's not what's going on. Listen to the way *do* and *don't* are pronounced: they don't have anything like the same vowel sound. And the *-n't* form of *Will* is *won't*. And *mustn't* is pronounced without the *t* sound of *must*. Irregularities of this kind signal that these aren't contractions at all; they're irregular inflected forms of verbs, just like past tenses (notice, *sent* isn't a contracted pronunciation of *sended*!).

• Auxiliary verbs can stand at the beginning of certain clauses including **closed interrogatives**, but lexical verbs never do. The sentence *They can tune it* (meaning "They are able to tune it") has the auxiliary verb *Can* but *They can tuna* (meaning "They pack tuna into cans") has a lexical verb with the same spelling; and because only the first is an auxiliary verb, *Can they tune it?* is grammatical, but ~~Can they tuna?~~ is not. (You'd have to say *Do they can tuna?*, popping in the auxiliary *Do*.)

• The word *not* can follow an auxiliary to make the clause negative. In *We have washed the machine*, the word *have* is an auxiliary verb, but in *We have a washing machine*, the second word is a lexical verb meaning "own." Notice the contrast between *We have not washed the machine*, which is grammatical, and ~~We have not a washing machine~~, which isn't (because the *have* is the lexical verb meaning "possess").

Auxiliary *Be*

The profoundly strange verb *Be* has an extraordinary list of inflectional forms, nothing like that of any other verb. The gerund-participle form is predictable: you add *-ing* to the plain form and get *being*, and the past participle *been* has an unexpected pronunciation; but look at the other forms:

	NEUTRAL	NEGATIVE
1ST SINGULAR PRESENT TENSE:	*am*	—
3RD SINGULAR PRESENT TENSE:	*is*	*isn't*
PRESENT TENSE EVERYWHERE ELSE:	*are*	*aren't*
1ST AND 3RD SINGULAR PAST TENSE:	*was*	*wasn't*
PAST TENSE EVERYWHERE ELSE:	*were*	*weren't*

(The forms without the *-n't* are called neutral. We can't call them "positive," because a clause like *That is definitely not true* is a negative statement. The point is that *is* can be used in either a positive or a negative clause; *isn't* can only appear in a negative clause.)

Be is always an auxiliary, even when it's the only verb in a sentence (which shows that we shouldn't call auxiliaries "helping verbs" – some of them don't have another verb they can be said to help):

That guy is crazy.	[notice, there's only one verb here, namely *is*]
Is that guy crazy?	[verb in initial position – key sign of an auxiliary]
That guy isn't crazy.	[verb with -*n't* suffix – key sign of an auxiliary]
That guy is not crazy.	[verb with *not* after it – key sign of an auxiliary

What *Be* does

Be has several distinct uses that make it very important – in fact absolutely indispensable – to the grammar of English. Here are six of the constructions that make *Be* crucial:

- **Progressive aspect**: Almost any lexical verb can be used to indicate that an activity is currently in progress, by using *Be* plus a gerund-participle. *He makes a lot of noise* describes habitual rowdiness, but *He is making a lot of noise* describes noise-making continuing through a period including the present moment (but possibly temporary). *He built a house* describes a past accomplishment now over and done with, while *He was building a house* describes an activity (possibly never completed) that was in progress during some period in the past. Verbs that denote a non-temporary state without time boundaries are not used in the progressive: no one would say *She is knowing the answer* because we don't imagine a state of knowledge as potentially coming to an end.
- **Predication**: A standard way to say that someone exhibits a certain quality is to use *Be* followed by an adjective phrase: *Mary is extremely clever.* (Some other verbs can be used in a similar way: *Mary seems extremely clever.*)

- **Location**: A standard way to say that someone or something is in a certain location specified by some **Preposition Phrase** (PP) is to use *Be* before it: *George is in the kitchen.*
- **Identity**: The simplest way to assert the identity of one person with another uses *Be* before an NP: *Superman is really Clark Kent.*
- **Roles**: A very common way to say that someone has a certain role in society uses *Be* before an NP naming the role (often with no determiner): *Professor Nesbit is dean of the college.*
- **Passives**: The construction called the passive clause (see chapter 14) often involves a form of *Be* plus a past participle: *Hawaiian wildlife has been decimated by feral cats.*

Auxiliary *Do*

The lexeme that I'll call *Do*_{aux} has a very curious property: it's only ever found in places where having an auxiliary verb is obligatory. For example, to form a closed interrogative corresponding to a given declarative clause (compare *Lunch will be ready soon* with *Will lunch be ready soon?*), you MUST have an auxiliary before the subject. If you haven't got one (as with *They opened on time*), you have to use *Do*_{aux} (*Did they open on time?*). You have to use it even if the verb is the lexical one denoting an action, as in *Do your homework*, which we can call *Do*_{lex}: the closed interrogative is *Did you do your homework?*, with one occurrence of *Do*_{aux} and one of *Do*_{lex}.

Auxiliary *Have*

*Have*_{aux} is used when forming a clause talking about a completed past action from a standpoint where it has relevance to the present. It is followed by a verb in the past participle form. *The milk went sour* talks about a single event in the past, but *The milk has gone sour* talks about a similar event that happened in the past but has present relevance. Notice how *Elvis appeared in many films* is unremarkable but $^?$*Elvis has appeared in many films* sounds strange. (He died in 1977, so the present relevance assumption clashes with what we know.) You need to use *Have*$_{aux}$ even when the lexical verb is the other verb with that spelling, meaning "own" or "possess": <u>*Have*</u> *you* <u>*had*</u> *this rash for more than a week?* contains *Have*$_{aux}$ at the beginning and the past participle of *Have*$_{lex}$ after the subject. This can lead to a sequence of identical words: *I* <u>*had had*</u> *the rash for several weeks* contains the past tense of *Have*$_{aux}$ followed by the past participle of *Have*$_{lex}$.

Modal auxiliaries

The remaining auxiliaries are a strange bunch called the modal auxiliaries. Here's the list of neutral and negative forms for the six most basic ones:

	PRESENT NEUTRAL	PRESENT NEGATIVE	PAST NEUTRAL	PAST NEGATIVE
Can	can	can't, cannot	could	couldn't
May	may	—	might	mightn't
Must	must	mustn't	—	—
Ought	ought	oughtn't	ought	oughtn't
Shall	shall	$^?$shan't	should	shouldn't
Will	will	won't	would	wouldn't

Notice the various gaps, a sign of highly irregular verbs: *May* has no negative form; *Can* has two of them, the ordinary *can't* and the formal-style *cannot*; *Must* doesn't have any past tense forms; and there are other peculiarities.

None of the modals show the *s* suffix found on other verbs in the present tense with a 3rd-person singular subject. And another weirdness is that modals have only present and past tense forms: there are no participles, so we don't find ~~musted~~ or ~~maying~~. There's no plain form either, which is why you can say *I would like to be able to* but not ~~I would like to could~~.

Some of these strange animals are rare or even drifting into extinction, despite having been so common and basic to English for so long. The form *mayn't* occurred until about a hundred years ago but is dead now; *mightn't* and *oughtn't* still hang on in older people's usage but younger speakers hardly ever use them. **Shall** still occurs in offers to do things (*Shall I do it for you?*) and in conservative legal language (*No state shall pass any law impairing the obligation of contract*), but it's four hundred times rarer than **Will**. And the present tense negative form *shan't* has become virtually extinct in American English since the First World War: in 44 million words of American newspaper text I found 14,000 occurrences of *won't* but only two of *shan't*, both in columns written by Vermont Royster, who was born in 1914!

The form *should* originated as the past tense counterpart of *shall*. An early 20th-century novelist putting *I expect that I shall be needed at the office* into a past tense context would write *I expected that I should be needed at the office*, but today it would be vastly more common to use the lexeme **Will**, for which the past tense form is *would*.

A handful of other marginal items share the syntax of modals, and show similar variation between speakers: <u>Dare</u> we tell her?; <u>Need</u> we tell her?; We <u>had</u> better tell her; <u>Would</u> you rather I didn't tell her?; John <u>is</u> to be summoned immediately. . . The underlined items are like rare animals that have almost died out. And the more you look at the details of how they are used and what they mean and how their grammatical properties vary and overlap, the more amazing it seems that people can learn how to use them.

The core meanings of modals

Most of the modal auxiliaries have meanings that at root can be related to one of two broad notions: (i) possibility or permission, and (ii) necessity or obligation.

Can and **May** both talk about either the possibility of some occurrence or the freedom to do something. *Can* very often expresses simple capability: *You can get it if you really try* says you have the ability to get it; *It can rain even in the desert* says the conditions capable of making rain possible are found even in the desert. But *Can* also very often conveys permission, as in *You can go now*. (Do not trust the people who tell you that *Can* should never be used in the permission sense. They are saying that *Can I kiss you?* means "Do I have the physical ability to kiss you?" – which would mean the answer must be "Yes" unless it's uttered by someone who can't move. *Can I kiss you?* is virtually always asking for permission, and you can say no!)

May is often used to describe something as possibly true in the sense of being compatible with everything we know: *There may be chemical elements we haven't yet discovered* or *There may be no integer solutions to this equation*. But it is also commonly used to give permission: *You may kiss me now*.

The other modals mostly express the logical opposite of these notions: necessity, compulsion, requirement, or obligation.

- *Must*: *There must be something wrong with the mechanism* means it cannot possibly be working correctly, necessarily there is some fault; *You must try harder* either orders or urges you to try harder, because in some way that's necessary.
- *Need*: *You needn't wear shoes* means there's no necessity for footwear.
- *Ought*: This modal is often used when talking about moral or ethical obligations: *You ought to be more careful* means there's a duty or obligation on you to be more careful.
- *Shall*: *We shall overcome* expresses a firm prediction of victory. Using the past tense form (*should*) softens the assertion a bit, rather than referring to past time: *We should be all right* means we are probably going to be all right, given current knowledge. But somewhere along the way,

should developed a totally different meaning, perhaps best regarded as a separate lexeme **Should**: a sentence like *You should be more careful* has roughly the meaning "You ought to be more careful," and is only historically related to **Shall**. It's still a variety of necessity, but a weak one – the necessity comes from some sort of moral or practical obligation.

- **Will**: *You will do as I say* conveys that you have no choice, mainly because I'm commanding you, and *I will get this done* expresses an inner determination to get it done. (Notice the noun **Will**$_N$ as used to refer to the inner capacity of guiding your own actions.)

Referring to the future

Will is overwhelmingly most used for signaling reference to a future time, as in *The bus will leave soon* (which doesn't imply any inner determination on the part of the bus). Traditional grammars call that the future tense, but they're wrong: it isn't a tense. English actually uses a whole slew of different combinations of words to talk about the future with different degrees of immediacy, but none of them are like tenses. Alongside *The bus will leave soon* we find *The bus leaves soon*; *The bus is leaving soon*; *The bus is to leave soon*; *The bus is set to leave soon*; *The bus is going to leave soon*; *The bus is about to leave*; *The bus is on the point of leaving*; and so on.

Because the past tense form of **Will** is *would*, it provides a way of talking about a time in the past that was in future time relative to an earlier time in the past, like this:

They told me at 7:55 that the bus would leave at 8:05, and it's now 8:15.

Would is the past tense of *will* in its future-time meaning. What the guy at the information desk said was "The bus will leave at 8:05," and we're talking about the future as defined relative to when he said it (7:55); by 8:15, that future is in the past. If you think that through, it does make sense. But I wouldn't call such subtleties of meaning simple, and I've hardly scratched the surface of them in this short chapter.

8

Adjectives

The **adjectives** are the words providing most of the simplest ways of referring to static properties: temporary or permanent states or conditions that people or things can be in. They include words like *Anxious, Bold, Childish, Deceptive, Eager, Furtive, Great, High, Interesting, Jaunty, Keen, Loose, Marvelous, New, Old, Public, Quiet, Realistic, Shady, Tremulous, Unfortunate, Vicious, Wild, Xenophobic, Young, Zesty,* and thousands more.

A huge proportion of them have **gradable** meanings, which means they name properties that something can have to a greater or lesser degree. These can take intensifying modifiers like *highly* or *extremely,* or the extremely frequent extent-increasing adverb *very*: we find *very anxious, very bold, very childish, very deceptive, very eager,* and so on. The adverb *very* provides a good test for adjectives: if it occurs modifying a word, you can bet that that word is an adjective. (Don't be confused by the adjective with the same spelling, which you see in phrases like *the very person I was looking for.* That word means something like "exact," and it is not gradable, so you can't repeat it for emphasis: we get *very, very anxious* but not ~~*the very, very person I was looking for.*~~)

Adjectives don't show tense or agreement forms, so there is no past tense of *anxious*; the tense in *She was anxious* is expressed in the verb form *was*.

The chaos of the traditional definition

Adjectives are traditionally defined as words that have the function of modifying nouns, or even more vaguely as "describing" words. These definitions are hopeless: not all adjectives function as noun modifiers, and lots of other words can serve that function. The common noun *bus* modifies the noun *station* in the phrase *bus station*; the proper noun *California* modifies the noun *girls* in *California girls*; participles of verbs like *written* or *sleeping* modify nouns in *written materials* or *sleeping dogs*). Talking about modifying nouns casts the net far too wide. Worse, determinatives like *All*, *An*, and *The* occur before nouns and sort of modify them, so under the traditional view all the determinatives also get included among the adjectives.

In fact most words in the language can be adjectives under the traditional definition, so the concept gets completely lost. Adjectives need to be separated out more carefully: they often have the function of modifying nouns, but not everything that modifies a noun is an adjective!

Inflected forms of adjectives

Many of the commonest adjective lexemes in English, especially the shorter ones, take endings that signal **comparison**. The **positive** form of the lexeme takes no ending: *The Moncktons are rich*. The **comparative** form takes the ending *-er*, used to signal having the property to a greater degree than other things they're being compared with: *The Moncktons are richer than our family*. And the *-est* ending yields the **superlative** form, signaling having the property to the maximum degree, like ranking first in some set: *The Moncktons are the <u>richest</u> people in town.* So we have sets of forms like this:

LEXEME	POSITIVE	COMPARATIVE	SUPERLATIVE
Bold:	bold	bolder	boldest
Deep:	deep	deeper	deepest
Easy:	easy	easier	easiest
Grand:	grand	grander	grandest
Happy:	happy	happier	happiest

The adjectives that take these endings are typically quite short – most have fewer than three syllables. They include **Angry, Bold, Calm, Deep, Easy, Fresh, Grand, Happy, Idle, Jaunty, Keen, Loose, Mild, New, Old, Pretty, Quiet, Rare, Shady, Tight, Ugly, Vast, Wild, Young, Zippy,** and lots of others.

With a few adjectives the non-positive forms have an unexpected irregular shape:

LEXEME	POSITIVE	COMPARATIVE	SUPERLATIVE
Bad:	bad	worse	worst
Far:	far	farther	farthest
Good:	good	better	best

Longer and more complex adjectives (and that's most of them) don't take these inflections: we never find ~~attractiver~~, ~~childisher, picturesquer, enjoyablest, fabulousest, interestingest~~, or anything of the sort. So how do we get around that to express comparisons? By using the items *more* and *most*: we use *more attractive* rather than ~~attractiver~~, *the most attractive* rather than ~~the attractivest~~, and so on.

Phrases like *more attractive* and *the most attractive* are **Adjective Phrases (AdjPs)**. *More* and *most* serve as **modifiers**. Many other items, often adverbs, can serve as modifiers in AdjPs: *very attractive, so careful, more important, extremely kind,* and so on.

AdjPs can serve in four different kinds of function (that is, they can do four different kinds of job in a sentence). These examples illustrate the four functions in which an adjective phrase headed by *Attractive* can serve as:

- **attributive modifier** in an NP: *It was* [$_{NP}$ *a very attractive design*].
- **predicative complement** in a VP: *The design* [$_{VP}$ *looked very attractive*].
- **postpositive modifier** in an NP: *Try to create* [$_{NP}$ *something really attractive*].
- **external modifier** of an NP with the indefinite article: *I'd never seen* [$_{NP}$ *so attractive a design*].

The rich and the poor

If phrases like *the poor* or *the French* are noticed at all in traditional grammars, they will probably be described as showing that adjectives can be "used as nouns," which is completely wrong. They don't behave anything like nouns. Nouns have plurals, but you can't call poverty-stricken people ~~poors~~, or call French people ~~Frenches~~. These phrases clearly have a definite article and an adjective and nothing else.

What's more, when the adjective has a gradable meaning, as *poor* does, you can precede it with the adjective-modifying adverb *very*, and talk about *the very poor* (or *the very, very poor*). What's going on is that there's a special extra possibility for attributive adjectives: when you're referring to the whole class of human beings who have a certain property, you can use the definite article plus an attributive adjective denoting the property, and it counts grammatically as a whole plural NP. We see the same thing in phrases like *the good, the bad, and the ugly*. In effect, the adjective serves as modifier and head at the same time in these phrases.

A very few adjectives actually do get used as nouns. It's useful to compare **Grateful** with **Hopeful**. People who thank you cannot be called ~~gratefuls~~, because **Grateful** is an adjective. But we do refer to *presidential hopefuls* around election time. The *s* ending on *hopefuls* tells you that the word can be a noun as well as an adjective. Most adjectives don't get converted into nouns, but this one managed it.

For many nationalities there are nouns naming the people of the country: we can talk about Americans, Germans, Icelanders, Israelis, Russians, and so on. When nouns are available, we use them. But for countries like the UK, France, the Netherlands, Switzerland, China, Japan, there isn't a convenient noun. Using *Frenchmen* sounds as if it only covers the men, and *Chinamen* seems vaguely insulting as well as old-fashioned. So we use the special attributive adjective construction instead: *the British, the French, the Dutch, the Swiss, the Chinese, the Japanese.*

NPs of this type are plural (that's why we say *The poor <u>are</u> always with us*, not *~~The poor is always with us~~*), and they refer solely to human beings (*The Swiss are wonderful* is about people, not wristwatches). But that still doesn't mean the adjective has turned into a plural human-referring noun; what we're looking at is simply a special thing you can do to make plural NPs using adjectives.

There's a similar but not so common construction with abstract concepts, a bit literary in flavor. You can say *the unthinkable* to refer to all the stuff that one can't bear to think about; you can refer to black magic, spiritualism, and so on, as *the occult*; you can call the entire class of things you never thought would happen as *the unexpected*. These are singular NPs referring to abstract notions, but again, just because they have the special property of lacking a head noun, that doesn't mean the adjectives are being "used as nouns." They aren't: ~~We faced many unexpecteds~~ is ungrammatical because you can't put the plural *s* on an adjective. Only a few adjectives, like *unknown*, really have developed uses as nouns; the plural *unknowns* in the celebrated phrase *There are unknown unknowns* proves it.

Complements in Adjective Phrases

Just like verbs, adjectives form phrases (AdjPs) with complements following the head. These complements are nearly always Preposition Phrases (PPs) or clauses:

proud of her achievements	(*of*-PP complement)
content with his present job	(*with*-PP complement)
kind to animals	(*to*-PP complement)
aghast at the prospect of moving	(*at*-PP complement)
glad that no one had seen us	(full clause complement)
eager to assist you	(subjectless clause complement)

Different adjectives take different sorts of complement, so a complete dictionary would need to say for each adjective what kind of complement it takes. You can't say ~~proud to her achievements~~, because the lexeme **Proud** demands a PP complement with *of* as its head; we don't find ~~content to his present job~~ because **Content** requires a PP headed by *with*; you can't write ~~kind that no one had seen us~~ because **Kind** doesn't take a clause complement; and so on.

Which adjectives take which prepositions? Bad news: it's not fixed by meaning or logic, so you can't use common sense and it will do no good to guess. When in doubt, then, check with some reliable reference work such as the *Longman Dictionary of Contemporary English*, or if necessary just see what other people write. Google a suitable phrase, and see if your guess matches what other people have written. When I put this into the Google search box (complete with the quotation marks):

```
"proud to her achievements"
```

I got a message saying, "It looks like there aren't many great matches for your search." But then I tried this instead:

```
"proud of her achievements"
```

That got me the message "About 212,000 results." Now, raw figures from Google searches are usually not much use as data (the estimates come from a quick skim of the first few hundred items in Google's index of the web, and they're often inaccurate), but the difference between 212,000 and virtually none does give you a hint about which choice you should make!

9

Adverbs

All that writing instructors seem to want to tell you about adverbs is that you should seek them out in your writing and eliminate them. "Write with nouns and verbs, not adjectives and adverbs," said E.B. White (though he doesn't, and nobody else does either). "Most adverbs are unnecessary," wrote William Zinsser (sure, if you don't care about what your sentences mean). Stephen King goes so far as to assert that "the road to hell is paved with adverbs." His next adverb came just twenty-eight words later, so he's on the road to hell.

The people who say these things never follow their own advice. They could hardly carry on writing if they did. Between 5 and 10 percent of the words in almost anything that a normal person writes will be adverbs. Reducing your adverb count to zero is a ridiculous goal, and there's no point in trying to attain it.

(After writing and rewriting the two paragraphs above to say what I wanted, I naturally decided to check my own writing, so I went through and counted the adverbs. A shade over 6.6 percent of the word count; perfectly normal.)

Identifying adverbs

Often the people who warn you off adverbs don't know how to identify them. And no wonder if they use the traditional descriptions, because they do an appallingly bad job of definition. The basic idea is supposed to be that any word that modifies or qualifies words other than nouns is an adverb. Traditional grammars say that although the word *up* in the sentence *The kitten climbed up the tree* is a preposition (see chapter 10), it's entirely different from the word *up* in *The kitten climbed up*. There they call it an adverb. So they're saying English has two distinct words with the same spelling (coincidence number one!) and the same pronunciation (number two!) and the same meaning (number three!). It's a clumsy and inelegant hypothesis.

I'll ignore the inexplicable traditional practice (though all printed dictionaries that I know of follow it): I'll treat *up* as a preposition in both uses.

Setting aside the falsely identified adverbs that are really prepositions, we can divide the category of adverbs in English into two unequal groups: first, there's a small class of basic adverbs. This list of three dozen basic adverb lexemes contains most of them:

Again	*Almost*	*Aloud*	*Already*
Also	*Altogether*	*Always*	*Anyhow*
Anyway	*Doubtless*	*Else*	*Even*
Ever	*However*	*Indeed*	*Just*
Likewise	*Maybe*	*Moreover*	*Nevertheless*
Not	*Often*	*Perhaps*	*Please*
Quite	*Rather*	*Right*	*Seldom*
So	*Soon*	*Still*	*Though*
Too	*Very*	*Why*	*Yet*

One or two of these have the same spelling as other words in different categories. For example, there's an adjective *even* as in *the even numbers*, which is distinct from the adverb in *Don't even try*. If and when it ever matters, I'll assign unambiguous lexeme names to the ambiguous items: for example, I might use **Even**$_{adj}$ for the adjective and use **Even**$_{adv}$ for the adverb.

But the rest of the adverbs – thousands and thousands of them, a huge majority – are formed by adding *-ly* to the plain form of an adjective, with a predictable meaning that generally relates to the manner in which something is done: **Anxiously** ("in an anxious way"), **Boldly** ("in a bold way"), **Childishly** ("in a childish way"), **Deceptively** ("in a deceptive way"), **Eagerly** ("in an eager way"), **Furtively** ("in a furtive way"), . . . You can extend the list all the way down to **Zealously**, though you'll find that sometimes the meaning of an *-ly* adverb is unexpected: **Great** means "very large or very good" but **Greatly** means "very much"; **High** means "way up off the ground" but **Highly** means "very"; **Large** means "big" but **Largely** means "mostly"; and so on.

Some adjectives don't form adverbs with *-ly*: we don't encounter adverbs like ~~asleeply~~, ~~bigly~~, ~~coloredly~~, ~~deafly~~, ~~exemptly~~, ~~fatly~~, ~~goldenly~~, and you could probably extend this list all the way down to ~~zodiacally~~. The gaps seem to be mostly explained by the meanings: the adjective *cautious* naturally yields an adverb *cautiously* because you can envisage doing things in a manner describable as cautious. You can't really imagine doing something in a manner describable as asleep, or big, or colored.

A small number of *-ly* adverbs are based on nouns instead of adjectives (*bodily, chiefly, partly, purposely*, and a few others).

The ending *-ly* is not an infallible diagnostic for adverbs: some words ending in *-ly* are adjectives (**Early, Jolly, Ugly, Weekly**) and others are nouns or verbs.

Uses of adverbs

Adverbs function as modifiers for verbs, adjectives, prepositions, determinatives, or other adverbs, and occasionally even
nouns. In the following examples, the adverb is in bold and the
head word that it modifies is underlined:

EXAMPLE	WHAT GETS MODIFIED
*The remaining forces <u>resisted</u> **strongly**.*	verb
*Their house was **extremely** <u>small</u>.*	adjective
*This piano is **completely** <u>out</u> of tune.*	preposition
*There were **hardly** <u>any</u> nuts left.*	determinative
*The water was **quite** <u>unnecessarily</u> hot.*	adverb
*The <u>news</u> **recently** that he had died shocked us.*	noun

It's a bad failing of virtually all traditional books on grammar
that they often confuse the **category** of adverbs with the
function of being a modifier. Any phrase that seems to modify
a verb, adjective, preposition, determinative, or adverb is
likely to be called an adverb (or an "adverbial," a thoroughly
unhelpful term that I avoid). So when they notice that *She
left in haste* has roughly the same meaning as *She left hastily,*
they call *in haste* either an adverb or an "adverbial." This is a
mistake: *in haste* is grammatically a PP, with the preposition *in*
as its head. Its **function** is that of modifier of a verb, but that's
not the same thing as being an adverb.

Adverb Phrases

Adverbs do form adverb phrases, though. Typically an Adverb
Phrase (AdvP) has a head adverb modified by another adverb:
very carefully, quite sufficiently, almost completely are AdvPs
where the second word is the head. But in addition, a few

adverbs take PP complements of particular types. In these examples, the underlined part is an AdvP consisting of an adverb and its PP or clause complement:

> *The subsidiary operates <u>independently of the rest of the company</u>.*
> *The lions are housed <u>separately from the tigers</u>.*
> *<u>Fortunately for you</u>, no one was killed.*

Bare adverbs and informal style

There are some basic adverbs that happen to have exactly the same shape as their related adjectives for all speakers, like the underlined ones here:

> *The mail arrived <u>late</u>.*
> *Hit that nail <u>hard</u>.*
> *You have to dig <u>deep</u>.*
> *It had seldom flown so <u>high</u>.*

But it's a familiar fact about American English that speakers of non-standard dialects (and Standard English speakers when speaking informally) extend the pattern to quite a few other adverbs. It's there in at least three Elvis Presley song titles (*Love me <u>tender</u>, Treat me <u>nice</u>,* and *Kiss me <u>quick</u>*), and lots of other songs (like the Beatles' *Hold me <u>tight</u>*). And in colloquial non-standard American English you will hear uses like these:

> *Drink it <u>slow</u> now, you hear?*
> *Tom slapped him <u>good</u>.*
> *You're ugly and your mom dresses you <u>funny</u>.*
> *I slept so <u>sound</u> in that big bed.*
> *It come up <u>real</u> <u>nice</u> when we polished it.*

I've been told by more than one educated person who has noticed non-standard expressions like these that adverbs are disappearing altogether from American English. That's completely untrue; the phenomenon is not that general. For one thing, it only applies to adverbs following the verb in a VP. Nobody says ~~Quite frank I don't care~~ to mean *Quite frankly I don't care*. Nobody says ~~He had evident embellished his resumé~~ when they mean *He had evidently embellished his resumé*. You never find people saying ~~The whole thing was beautiful done~~ when they meant *The whole thing was beautifully done*. So we shouldn't exaggerate the very limited use of bare adverbs in colloquial American speech.

One minor problem associated with this topic is that some people, having been warned off the informal-style use of bare adverbs, overcompensate by sticking *-ly* where it isn't called for. You get people writing *thusly*, for example (the adverb is *thus*, and doesn't need the *-ly*). And some people put *-ly* on adjectives in expressions like ~~I feel badly~~ (the verb **Feel** takes predicative AdjP complements, so the expected version is *I feel bad*).

To summarize, the adjective/adverb distinction gets a little bit blurred here and there, and there are style considerations regarding some familiar American English usages. It shouldn't be exaggerated, though: adjectives and adverbs are still clearly distinguishable.

Adverbophobia

That leads us to the puzzling phenomenon of all the warnings in the how-to-write books. Why do they fear adverbs so much? The reason seems to be that they are worried that if you were ever left to write as you wish you would use adverbs too much, in contexts where you could have avoided them. They think you'll rely on sticking in modifiers instead of choosing better verbs and adjectives in the first place.

For example, they seem to imagine you might write *very big* instead of *huge*; *really bad* instead of *evil*; *rudely took it* instead of *snatched it*; *read it hastily* instead of *skimmed it*; *grossly overweight* instead of *obese*; *terribly frightened* instead of *petrified*; *greedily drank the wine* instead of *guzzled the wine*; and so on. I don't know why this is perceived as such an awful danger, but that appears to be the worry, and writing teachers have told me they see such phrases far too much in student essays.

Well, it is my duty to warn you that the advice about avoiding adverbs is mistaken, for two rather obvious reasons.

The first reason is that you can't normally get rid of an adverb by making a better choice of verb, adjective, or whatever, because there just isn't one. You can't avoid the adverb *rapidly* in a sentence like *It rapidly corroded* by finding a verb that means "undergo corrosion in a short space of time"; you can't eliminate the adverb *permanently* in an adjective phrase like *permanently ineligible* by choosing a better adjective than *ineligible*, one that has the no-time-limit part of the meaning baked in. You can't get rid of the adverb *seldom* in a sentence like *He seldom wrote to her* by choosing a verb that means the same as **Write** but signals that it wasn't very often.

And the second reason for not recommending avoidance of adverbs is that even if some inexperienced writers use adverbs where they didn't need to (perhaps where they're redundant, or maybe just to increase the word count of a required paper), that doesn't mean everyone else should be told to do without adverbs all the time! Suppose it's true that some dimwit tends to write *He shouted loudly*, not realizing that shouting is always loud, or writes *We hurried off quickly* because of a failure to understand what hurrying is. That shouldn't be allowed to ruin it for the rest of us! If I choose to write *He lingered uneasily* or *She responded bitterly*, it's nobody's business but mine, and I don't want purported writing experts telling me to take those adverbs out simply because of adverbophobia.

You should just ignore most of what the how-to-write books say about this category of words. Adverbs are a familiar feature of everybody's writing. Stephen King asserts that the road to hell is paved with adverbs, but the moment he gets back to doing what he's good at – writing stories of suspense and horror – he uses adverbs at will, just like the rest of us. In fact somewhat more. I checked quite a few pages of his writing, and around 8 percent was typical for him, both before and after he published *On Writing*. The first adverb in *Insomnia* (1994) is in line 1; the first one in *Under the Dome* (2009) is in line 3. Check for yourself. (Notice, by the way, that if I followed the traditional definition, the adverb count in everyone's prose would be higher. The count in my first two paragraphs above would be nearly 10 percent, and Stephen King would be much closer to eternal torment.)

Adverbs aren't going away, and you shouldn't be ashamed of using them when you need them. The blanket elimination instruction you find in too many how-to-write books and websites is absurd. Indisputably absurd.

10

Prepositions

All English dictionaries in print that I know of give a mistaken account of **prepositions**. They muddle prepositions together with adverbs and with what they call "conjunctions," because they're following the bad precedents of traditional grammars. In this chapter I'll break away from the muddle and inaccuracy of the last few hundred years. A side effect of doing this will be to reveal that English actually has far more prepositions than the old-fashioned books assume.

The most basic and frequent prepositions are short words that take NP complements. The meanings they express quite often have to do with location in time or space. A preposition plus its complement makes a **Preposition Phrase** or **PP**. I'll sometimes refer to different kinds of PP according to what they have as their head preposition: a PP with *of* as its head will be an *of*-PP, and so on.

Some prepositions take **obligatory** NP complements. I underline the PP in each of these examples, and show you the ungrammatical result of leaving the preposition out:

She's <u>at school</u>.   ~~She's at.~~
Get <u>into the car</u>.   ~~Get into.~~

I took a photo <u>of you</u>.	~~*I took a photo of.*~~
Do one favor <u>for me</u>.	~~*Do one favor for.*~~
This came <u>from India</u>.	~~*This came from.*~~
I'm <u>with her</u>.	~~*I'm with.*~~

The grammar books of the 18th and 19th centuries talked as if all prepositions were like these: they DEFINE prepositions as words standing before a noun (by which they meant an NP) and signaling a relation in space or time to something else in the sentence. That's a big mistake. First, many prepositions can occur either with or without an NP:

They went right <u>by it</u>.	*They went right <u>by</u>.*
He fell <u>down the stairs</u>.	*He fell <u>down</u>.*
Just jump <u>off the roof</u>.	*Just jump <u>off</u>.*
I can't get <u>in my room</u>.	*I can't get <u>in</u>.*
What's <u>on TV</u> tonight?	*What's <u>on</u> tonight?*
Go <u>round the corner</u> and collect it.	*Go <u>round</u> and collect it.*

Traditional grammars say that the underlined words in the right-hand column are adverbs (because they modify the verb, sort of). But these words don't behave anything like adverbs! Adverbs can often go before the verb, but the underlined words above don't:

My horse fell immediately.	*My horse fell down.*
My horse immediately fell.	~~*My horse down fell.*~~
The plumber fixed it promptly.	*The plumber fixed it up.*
The plumber promptly fixed it.	~~*The plumber up fixed it.*~~
I'll come soon and collect it.	*I'll come round and collect it*
I'll soon come and collect it.	~~*I'll round come and collect it.*~~

Calling *down* and *up* and *round* adverbs is a major mistake. How could grammarians blunder so badly? I don't know. It's true that people were wrong about all sorts of things in the first half of the 18th century. But by 1756 Linnaeus had decided to classify whales with mammals rather than with fish, whereas two hundred years later the same old nonsense about prepositions was still being repeated.

What's amazing is that the right description is so very simple: some prepositions take obligatory NP complements (just like the verb *get*, where *Let's get some pizza* is fine but ~~Let's get~~ is ungrammatical), while others take optional NP complements (just like the verb *eat*, where *Let's eat some pizza* is fine and so is *Let's eat*).

A natural question at this point would be whether there are any prepositions that are like the verb *elapse*, and take no complement at all, ever. And the answer is yes. To see this, note first that the word *right*, when it's a modifier of the following word, is entirely restricted to prepositions in contemporary Standard English (it's not true of all non-standard dialects):

~~The school is right convenient.~~	[*right* + adjective: not grammatical]
~~There is a school right locally.~~	[*right* + adverb: not grammatical]
~~The school right faces our house.~~	[*right* + adverb: not grammatical]
The school is right across the road.	[*right* + preposition: grammatical]

When you use the modifier *right* with any preposition that has a meaning relating to location in time or space, it contributes a sense of accuracy, as in *right on target* or *right on time*. And when the preposition has a directional meaning, *right* contributes a sense of complete traversal of some path (*She rode right into the town center* or *It lasted right into the summer*). And all of this works just as well with prepositions that take no NP complement:

That road doesn't go <u>right through</u> the park.
That road doesn't go <u>right through</u>.
It went <u>right down</u> the trash chute.
It went <u>right down</u>.

It also goes with prepositions that don't allow NP complements at all:

You should keep <u>right away</u>.
I'll be <u>right back</u>.
Let's hold the show <u>right here</u>!
Make sure you come <u>right home</u> afterwards.
Clean up your room, <u>right now</u>.
It happened <u>right there</u>.

So *away, back, here, home, now,* and *there* are all best regarded as prepositions, not adverbs!

Another defect of the traditional account of prepositions becomes apparent when we consider words like *after, before,* and *since.* These often take clauses as their complements. Because of this, every printed dictionary I know about calls them "subordinating conjunctions." But it's crazy to think that in the following sentences we have three different words, all of them spelled *before,* and all meaning basically the same thing, but differing in category:

I'd never seen him <u>before that fight</u>.	[NP complement]
I'd never seen him <u>before we had that fight</u>.	[clause complement]
I'd never seen him <u>before</u>.	[no complement]

It's similarly irrational to think that in the following sentences we really have three different words, all spelled *since* and all having the same basic meaning:

I've loved her ever <u>since our first meeting</u>.	[NP complement]
I've loved her ever <u>since we first met</u>.	[clause complement]
I've loved her ever <u>since</u>.	[no complement]

I'm not the first person to point this out, by the way. It was argued by John Hunter in a paper presented to the Royal Society of Edinburgh in 1784. But the tradition endured for another 240 years, with only a few linguists realizing what the sensible explanation would be: prepositions, like verbs, take various kinds of complement, and one possibility is a clause.

This yields an answer to the question of how to classify words like *although, until,* and the conditional *if* seen in *Take it if you want it*: these are prepositions that ALWAYS take clause complements.

Prepositions can also take PP complements (again, much like verbs). Look at the underlined phrases in these examples:

> *Keep the flowers <u>away from the candle</u>.*
> <u>*According to this website*</u>*, aliens built the pyramids.*
> *The land is more level <u>east of the river</u>.*
> *They had to cancel the trip <u>because of the fog</u>.*
> *She carefully lifted it <u>out of the box</u> and held it up.*

Away, according, east, because, and *out* are prepositions taking PP complements, and each one demands a specific head preposition in its complement. *Away* requires a PP headed by *from*; *according* needs a PP complement with the head *to*; *east* takes *of*; and so on.

There are some slight dialect variations. In colloquial American speech (but not British), *out* takes NP complements denoting exits from enclosed spaces, as in *He ran <u>out the door</u>,* and has *of*-PP complements with *off, inside,* and *outside* (e.g. *Get this thing <u>off of me</u>*). In a still rather jocular use, *because* has started occurring with NP complements, as in *I must photograph this salad – <u>because Instagram</u>!* But none of this necessitates consigning any of these words to different categories. We're just looking at a few idiosyncrasies regarding what head prepositions are needed in the PP complements of prepositions.

There are actually over 250 prepositions in English, though some may not be familiar to everyone (like Scottish *anent* or *outwith*). On page 82 I give an incomplete sample – just a select list of 160 words that are definitely best categorized as prepositions. Some are rare (*aslant*) or somewhat archaic (*unto*); some originated as participle forms of verbs (*including*); a few have been borrowed from French (*sans*) or Latin (*qua*); but most are common enough that nearly every user of English knows them.

aboard	*about*	*above*	*abreast*
abroad	*absent*	*according*	*across*
adrift	*aft*	*after*	*against*
ago	*ahead*	*akimbo*	*aloft*
along	*alongside*	*although*	*amid*
among	*apart*	*apropos*	*around*
as	*ashore*	*aside*	*aslant*
astride	*at*	*away*	*back*
bar	*barring*	*based*	*because*
before	*beforehand*	*behind*	*below*
beneath	*beside(s)*	*between*	*betwixt*
beyond	*but*	*by*	*chez*
circa	*come*	*contra*	*counting*
cum	*despite*	*down*	*due*
during	*east*	*ere*	*except*
excepting	*following*	*for*	*forth*
forward(s)	*from*	*given*	*granted*
hence	*henceforth*	*here*	*home*
if	*in*	*including*	*indoors*
inside	*instead*	*into*	*less*
lest	*like*	*minus*	*modulo*
near	*nearby*	*next*	*north*
now	*o'clock*	*of*	*off*
on	*once*	*onto*	*onward(s)*
opposite	*out*	*over*	*owing*
past	*pending*	*per*	*plus*
prior	*pro*	*provided*	*providing*
pursuant	*qua*	*regarding*	*respecting*
round	*sans*	*save*	*saving*
seeing	*short*	*since*	*so*
south	*sub*	*supposing*	*than*
then	*thence*	*thenceforth*	*there*
though	*through*	*throughout*	*till*
times	*to*	*together*	*toward(s)*
under	*underfoot*	*underground*	*underneath*
unless	*unlike*	*until*	*unto*
up	*upon*	*versus*	*via*
vis-à-vis	*wanting*	*west*	*when*
whence	*where*	*whereas*	*while*
whilst	*with*	*within*	*without*

11

Coordinators, subordinators, and interjections

The remaining categories of words I will need to refer to are very small. Two of them are very important: **coordinators** are vital for linking phrases and clauses together, and **subordinators** permit embedding a clause inside another clause. And that leaves the category of **interjections**, which are frequent in speech, but for grammatical purposes have only marginal importance.

Coordinators

The coordinators are a tiny class of words used to link words, phrases, or clauses on an equal footing. The main ones are *and*, *but*, *nor*, and *or*. (You'll find them referred to in traditional grammars as "coordinating conjunctions" or just "conjunctions.")

What I mean by linking on an equal footing is that in a sentence like the following, neither of the two underlined bits contains or dominates the other:

I'm not going to tidy my room and *I'm not going to take out the trash.*

The bit before *and* isn't a subordinate part of the bit after it. Nor the reverse. The two clauses just sit beside each other, equal in rank, each making its own rebellious assertion. In fact you can switch their order without changing meaning: *I'm not going to take out the trash* and *I'm not going to tidy my room* says exactly the same thing.

Linkage of this sort is called **coordination**, and I'll call the linked subparts **coordinates**.

The coordinates can be phrases rather than clauses: *Jack and Jill went up the hill* has NP coordinates (underlined), and has the same meaning as *Jill and Jack went up the hill*.

You can have a coordination with PP coordinates too: *It's either under the sink or in the cellar* has PP coordinates (again, they're underlined), and means exactly the same as *It's either in the cellar or under the sink*.

However, constituents of different categories can form a coordination provided their functions are the same. The coordinates in *The incident was off campus and relatively unimportant* are a PP and an AdjP, but both function as complements of the verb *Be*. American informal usage allows *It will arrive Friday or over the weekend*, where the coordinates are an NP and a PP, but notice that both are functioning as time adjuncts in the *arrive* clause.

Notice also that we get *He's a liberal and proud of it*, because either the NP *a liberal* or the AdjP *proud of it* could serve as a complement in that clause. However, we don't get *A liberal and proud of it would have voted the other way*, because although the NP *a liberal* would be allowed as the subject of *would have voted the other way*, the AdjP *proud of it* would not.

When a coordination of NPs has just two coordinates and the coordinator is *and*, the determinative *both* can appear before it (*both Jack and Jill*). When the coordinator is *or*, the determinative is *either* (*either Jack or Jill*). And regardless of how many coordinates there are, when the coordinator is *or*, you can put the determinative *either* in front of it to emphasize the fact that the coordinates present alternatives: *either toast, hash browns, or pancakes.*

There's a wealth of other complex facts about coordination that could be explored, and this little book can hardly even scratch the surface. For a start, coordinations with *but* are limited to two coordinates (a sentence like ~~I love you but she hates me but I love her~~ seems completely incoherent); yet coordinations with *and* or with *or* can have any number of coordinates, with the coordinator preceding just the last one (*For a Waldorf salad you need celery, walnuts, apples, grapes, and mayonnaise*) or repeated before all except the first (*celery and walnuts and apples and grapes and mayonnaise*).

Here I'll comment on just two recommendations that writing teachers make about coordinations.

The first is that although it's not that hard to find perfectly ordinary sentences with four or five or six coordinates, and occasionally writers produce sentences with dozens of coordinates, that is not normally recommended in serious writing. The teachers are right here. A succession of sentences linked in a long chain with *and* often seems like childish writing, so avoid it.

The other is that there are still English teachers and writing tutors around who think you shouldn't write a sentence beginning with a coordinator. They are wrong. No professional writer has ever respected that imaginary rule. Almost any kind of material you want to look at has sentences beginning with coordinators. In most novels the first sentence beginning with a coordinator will be on the first or second page, and others will soon follow it.

Subordinators

English has a tiny set of essentially meaningless words that mark the beginnings of certain subordinate clauses (that is, clauses contained inside larger clauses). I'll call these words **subordinators** (some linguists call them "complementizers," and traditional grammars call them "subordinating conjunctions" and wrongly throw a whole bunch of prepositions in with them). I'll discuss just three items that definitely have to be called subordinators.

That$_{sbr}$

Two completely different words share the spelling *that*. One is a determinative meaning something like "the one over there"; it rhymes with *cat* and is always stressed. I'll use the name *That*$_{det}$ for that one, which is irrelevant here. The other is the subordinator we're interested in. It's completely meaningless, it rhymes with the last syllable of *deli<u>cate</u>*, and it's virtually never stressed. I'll give it the name *That*$_{sbr}$, where "sbr" abbreviates "subordinator."

That$_{sbr}$ has two roles: it introduces **declarative content clauses** (see chapter 12), as in *I thought <u>that you didn't really care</u>*, and it introduces a certain kind of relative clause, as in *a car <u>that I'm really happy with</u>*.

Being meaningless, *That*$_{sbr}$ can often be omitted, though there are conditions. When a content clause immediately follows a verb, you can drop the subordinator:

> *I thought <u>that you didn't really care</u>.*
> *I thought <u>you didn't really care</u>.*

But you can't leave it out when the content clause is a subject:

> <u>*That no one really liked him*</u> *was well known.*
> ~~<u>No one really liked him</u> was well known.~~

That$_{sbr}$ can also be left off the beginning of a relative clause, but in Standard English it mustn't leave you with a clause beginning with a verb:

It's a car <u>that I'm really happy with</u>.
It's a car <u>I'm really happy with</u>.
It's a car <u>that appeals to me</u>.
~~*It's a car <u>appeals to me</u>.*~~

Whether

Whether introduces closed **interrogative content clauses,** as in *I wondered <u>whether anybody really cared</u>.* The underlined clause expresses the content of the question that *Does anybody really care?* would express as a full sentence. In slightly more informal style, it can be replaced by a meaningless *if,* which can be regarded as just a different shape for *whether* (it's not the conditional *if* seen in *If you want it you can have it*):

I wondered <u>whether anybody would listen</u>.
I wondered <u>if anybody would listen</u>.

But the *if* shape can't be substituted when the interrogative clause is a subject:

<u>*Whether anybody was listening*</u> *is the key question.*
~~<u>*If anybody was listening*</u> *is the key question.*~~

For_{sbr}

The spelling *for* most often stands for a preposition which we can call **For**_{prep}, as in *I bought a present for you,* but it's also the shape of a subordinator that we'll call **For**_{sbr}, which is used in sentences like:

Jim arranged <u>for us to be met at the airport</u>.

Here *for* is not a preposition; it's the subordinator that introduces infinitival clauses that have a subject NP.

The traditional muddle

It's very important that we get away from the traditional muddle, regrettably endorsed by all dictionaries in print that I know of, which assumes a much larger class of "subordinating conjunctions" embracing not just *That*~sbr~, *Whether*, and *For*~sbr~ but also a slew of words with very different properties that we've already considered: words like *after, although, because, before, if, lest, since, though, till, until, while,* and others. These words are all **prepositions** (see chapter 10), and the key thing that distinguishes them from subordinators is that they have real MEANINGS.

For example, *I'm happy that my ex is here* just says that my former partner is here and I'm okay with that. You could leave out the word *that*, because it adds nothing to the meaning. But *I'm happy because my ex is here* is strikingly different: it says the presence of my ex CAUSED my current happiness. And *I'm happy although my ex is here* says that my happiness survived DESPITE my ex showing up. The difference is crucial: prepositions like *because* and *although* make real meaning contributions, and subordinators like *that* don't.

Interjections

There is one remaining identifiable class of words in the dictionary not categorizable as nouns, verbs, adjectives, adverbs, prepositions, determinatives, subordinators, or coordinators: the **interjections**. They hardly fit into the structure of sentences at all. They're often used as single-word expressions of some sort of emotion or reaction, either as utterances on their own or as interruptions that can occur almost anywhere in a sentence. We're talking about words like these:

ah, ahem, aw, gah, gack, gee, gosh, ha, heck, hell, hello, hey, hi, hmm, huh, humph, hurrah, hush, oh, okay, ouch, phew, pooh, sheesh, shush, ugh, unh, well, whee, whoa, wow, yeah, yikes, yippee, yuck

Some are widely regarded as blasphemous (*Christ, damn, God, Jesus*) or obscene (*bugger, fuck, shit*); they're often called expletives and prim newspapers replace them by dashes or asterisks in reports of speech.

It would be a mistake to think of interjections as instinctive responses. They're words that you have to learn, and they need dictionary entries. Not everyone in the world says *Ouch!* if you step on their toe. And interjections can go out of style (like *zounds* or *golly*).

Though interjections frequently occur alone, that's not a diagnostic. Words of almost any category can occur as single-word reactions. An utterance can easily consist of just a verb (*Stop!*), a noun (*Idiot!*), an adjective (*Nice!*), adverb (*Never!*), pronoun (*What?*), preposition (*Down!*), or even a coordinator (*And?*). That doesn't make these words interjections.

The only things that interjections commonly combine with are NPs used in the construction where the NP denotes the addressee (it's often called the **vocative**): <u>Oh Mom</u>, *you're such a darling!*; <u>Gee, John</u>, *what were you thinking?*; *Hey, you, get off my lawn.*

The positive and negative words *yes* and *no* are probably best classified as interjections. They can in fact express momentary feelings or reactions (*Yes!* when your favorite tennis player makes a beautiful volley, or *No!* on seeing floodwater sweep away a car), but unlike the other interjections they can have an important logical function: *Yes* expresses a positive answer to a polar question, or agreement with a positive statement, while *No* expresses a negative answer, or a dissent.

12

Content clauses

Not all clauses in English are main clauses. The main clauses are the ones that could be used on their own as sentences. But declarative, interrogative, and exclamative clauses are capable of being embedded as subordinate subparts of larger clauses. (There isn't any such thing as an imperative content clause, though. Imperatives are inherently a main clause kind of thing.)

To be more specific, a verb, noun, adjective, adverb, or preposition that is the lexical head of a phrase can take a clause as a **complement** – and can impose a requirement regarding which kind of clause it will accept. In these examples, I underline the relevant lexical head and put the complement clause in square brackets:

> I _believed_ [that she has views like ours] until that speech yesterday.
> The _fact_ [that vaccines work] was treated as unproven propaganda.
> That thing was broken _before_ [I ever saw it], you know.

The bracketed clauses make vital contributions to the sentence, and contain separate information such as tense. In the first one, _believed_ is in the past tense, and _until that speech_ *yesterday* goes with it, but *she has views like ours* is a separate clause given in the present tense.

The bracketed parts are like main clauses in some ways, but not in every way: *that vaccines work* would not be allowed as a main clause; nor would *I ever saw it.* I'll call them **content clauses** from now on, because they express full sentence-like content of their own.

Sentences can have stacks of content clauses embedded in other content clauses. Take this sentence:

> *Jerry says*
> > [*that Susan thinks*
> > > [*the committee is going to decide*
> > > > [*that none of the applicants should be hired.*]]]

The part that says none of the applicants should be hired is a subpart of the clause about the committee's probable decision, which is a subpart of the clause describing Susan's opinion, which is a subpart of the clause describing what Jerry says, which is a subpart of the main clause.

Content clauses can also serve as subjects, if the predicate VP has the right sort of meaning – though a main clause with a clause as its subject may sound a bit ponderous:

> <u>*That our neighbors would go to all that trouble*</u> *makes me feel glad that I live here.*

Traditional grammars tend to call content clauses "noun clauses" because of a feeling that content clauses can serve as subjects and objects of verbs, just like nouns (by which they mean NPs). It's not a good parallel (verbs like ***Think*** and ***Inquire*** take content-clause complements but not NP complements), and I won't be using the term "noun clause" in this book.

Declarative content clauses

A declarative content clause can be the complement to a verb like **Believe** or **Think**, an adjective like **Happy** or **Glad**, a noun like **Fact** or **Idea**, or a preposition like **Since** or **Because**. It will look almost exactly like a declarative main clause, except that it may have the subordinator **That**$_{sbr}$ at the beginning. (The subordinator is sometimes optional, and is forbidden after most prepositions.) Some examples, with the content clause underlined:

LEXICAL HEAD	EXAMPLE
Think	We think <u>that they were careful</u>.
	We think <u>they were careful</u>.
Glad	We're glad <u>that they were so careful</u>.
	We're glad <u>they were so careful</u>.
Idea	We had no idea <u>that they were so careful</u>.
	We had no idea <u>they were so careful</u>.
Because	~~We trusted them because <u>that they were so careful</u>.~~
	We trusted them because <u>they were so careful</u>.

Interrogative content clauses

An interrogative content clause (like an interrogative main clause) can be closed or open. The closed ones begin with *whether* or *if*. The open ones begin with an interrogative word like *who* or *what*, and can follow various kinds of main clause word: a verb like **Wonder**, an adjective like **Unclear**, or a preposition such as **About**:

LEXICAL HEAD	EXAMPLE
Wonder	I wonder <u>whether they were careful</u>.
	I wonder <u>who they were talking to</u>.
Unclear	It's unclear <u>whether they were careful</u>.
	It's unclear <u>who they were talking to</u>.

LEXICAL HEAD	EXAMPLE
About	*I asked him about <u>whether they were careful</u>.*
	I asked him about <u>who they were talking to</u>.

The underlined subordinate clauses are of the interrogative type, though they don't look like main clause interrogatives: they don't have the auxiliary before the subject. They also differ in meaning: subordinate clauses like *whether they were careful* or *who they were talking to* don't actually ask questions, but you can see that their content is very close: to wonder whether they were careful is to reflect on what might be the correct answer to the question "Were they careful?" and to be unclear who they were talking to is to be unclear on how to give a correct answer to the question "Who were they talking to?"

Exclamative content clauses

Exclamative clauses can be content-clause complements as well: verbs like *Believe* and adjectives like *Amazing* can take them:

LEXICAL HEAD	EXAMPLE
Believe	*I can't believe <u>what an idiot he turned out to be</u>.*
Amazing	*It's amazing <u>how strong this stuff is</u>.*

What's being described as amazing in the second example, for instance, is not the answer to the question "How strong is this stuff?"; it's commenting on the sheer strength of the stuff, not asking about it.

13

Tenseless subordinate clauses

Tense isn't optional for main clauses in English: they must have tense. You can choose present tense (*bites*) or past tense (*bit*) in a main clause, but not a tenseless form like *bitten* or *biting*:

Your dog bites me.	[main clause with present tense – fine]
Your dog bit me.	[main clause with past tense – fine]
~~*Your dog bite me.*~~	[main clause with plain form verb – bad]
~~*Your dog biting me.*~~	[main clause with gerund-participle – bad]
~~*Your dog bitten me.*~~	[main clause with past participle – bad]

But in embedded clauses it's different: subordinate clauses can lack tense. In fact tenseless subordinate clauses are everywhere. They can be either declarative or interrogative, but because they often don't have subjects, it makes more sense to classify them according to the forms of their verbs rather than by clause type.

I'll deal first with the types of clause that require the **plain form** of the verb; then the clauses that require the **gerund-participial** form; and finally the ones that need the **past-participial** form. It's an interesting fact that all of them are to some extent associated with controversies about usage:

in this chapter we are going to tangle with the purists and grammar bullies more than we did in some others.

Clauses requiring the plain form

There are two kinds of clause in which the principal verb has to be in the plain form. I'll call them **mandative** and **infinitival**. And it will often be useful to illustrate them with *Be*, because it's the only verb that has a plain form completely different from all of its present tense forms: the plain form *be* is different from all the present tense forms *am, are,* and *is.*

Mandative clauses

In formal-style writing, and somewhat more in British than American English, verbs and adjectives of mandating (commanding, urging, requiring, etc., hence the name "mandative") take a minor type of subordinate clause that is always introduced by the subordinator *that,* and always has a subject, which if it's a pronoun will be in the nominative form (*I, he, she, we,* or *they*), but the clause has a plain form verb instead of a tensed verb:

> It is essential <u>that she be there promptly at noon.</u>
> I only ask <u>that the dog stay out of the bedroom.</u>
> The dean insisted <u>that I attend his stupid meeting.</u>

Those are good Standard English. However, lots of people substitute a tensed form for the plain form, so you will also find people writing in a more informal style, like this:

> It's essential <u>that she's there promptly at noon.</u>
> I only ask <u>that the dog stays out of the bedroom.</u>
> The dean insisted <u>that I attended his stupid meeting.</u>

Much of the time you won't be able to tell whether people are using the informal version or not, because the difference is only visible (or audible) when the verb is *Be* as in the first example, or the present tense is used and the subject is 3rd person as in the second, or the verb is in the past tense as in the third. So why would this special choice of verb form that lots of people don't use be worth mentioning here?

Because those who nitpick other people's grammar love to harp on this point. They will tell you that it is grammatically wrong to substitute the present tense, and that only the first group of examples above are formed correctly. This isn't true: the fully competent speakers and writers who say or write *It's essential that she's there* don't do it because they slipped up. But I thought I should warn you that the grammar bullies are waiting to sink their teeth into your ankle for not using the plain form in every mandative clause. (They often refer to the mandative type of clause as the "subjunctive.")

Some people worry that the informal version leads to ambiguity. They're not wrong about that: there's a possibility of ambiguity here. *Insist* has two meanings, one about emphatically claiming something is true and the other about demanding that someone should do something. *The dean insisted that I attend* has only the latter meaning (he required me to be there), but *The dean insisted that I attended*, which shares that meaning, can also mean he emphatically claimed that I actually WAS there. For people who would rather face a plague of locusts than permit an avoidable ambiguity, this is like having their underwear twisted.

You may think we should say to such people, "Get a life." By all means tell them that. I'm neither making these rules up nor trying to enforce them; my job in this book is to point out to you what seems to be the current state of the language and its speakers.

Infinitival clauses

Complement clauses with a plain form verb and optional subject are called **infinitival** clauses. Most are marked with a special infinitival marker spelled *to*, which is a separate word but is NOT the same word as the preposition with that spelling. I'll call them **to-infinitivals**. (Chapter 16 briefly discusses the old "split infinitive" myth that you mustn't put a word between *to* and the following verb, but for now, ignore it.)

There are also less common infinitivals that have just a bare plain form verb. I'll call them **bare infinitivals**. Many verbs, adjectives, or nouns specifically select infinitival clauses as their complements, either optionally or obligatorily. Here are some examples illustrating both types:

LEXICAL HEAD	EXAMPLE	
Try (verb)	We tried <u>to be careful</u>.	[*to*-infinitival]
Will (modal aux.)	We will <u>be careful</u>.	[bare infinitival]
Let (verb)	We let him <u>get away with it</u>.	[bare infinitival]
Happy (adjective)	I'll be happy <u>to help you</u>.	[*to*-infinitival]
Plan (noun)	Their plan <u>to keep it secret</u> failed.	[*to*-infinitival]

Verbs like *Try*, *Want*, *Hope*, *Love*, and lots of others take only *to*-infinitivals. Nearly all the modal auxiliaries take bare infinitival complements (*will* <u>be careful</u>, *must* <u>be careful</u>, *could* <u>be careful</u>, etc. – *Ought* is an exception, and takes a *to*-infinitival), and so do a few lexical verbs like *Let* and *See*. The unusual verb *Help* takes either a bare infinitival (*Help me* <u>move the piano</u>) or a *to*-infinitival (*Help me* <u>to move the piano</u>), and the even more unusual verb *Make* takes a bare infinitival in an active clause (*The voices in my head made me* <u>do it</u>) but a *to*-infinitival in a passive clause (*I was made* <u>to do it</u> *by the voices in my head*).

An infinitival clause can have the form of an interrogative, either closed or open:

LEXICAL HEAD	EXAMPLE	
Know (verb)	I didn't know <u>whether to believe them or not</u>.	(closed)
	I didn't know <u>who to talk to</u>.	(open)
Unclear (adjective)	It's unclear <u>whether to believe them</u>.	(closed)
	It's unclear <u>who to talk to</u>.	(open)

The underlined clauses are of the interrogative type, but with no subject and no tense, they don't look much like main clause interrogatives.

Infinitival clauses with subjects

A *to*-infinitival clause can have a subject. When it does, the subordinator *for* precedes the subject, as in *Jim arranged <u>for us to be met at the airport</u>*. The same kind of infinitival clause can be used as a subject: *<u>For someone to meet us at the airport</u> would be helpful*.

You might think that *for* could always be treated as a preposition, which is exactly how traditional grammars see it; but they're wrong. If *for him* were a PP in the airport examples, we'd have no explanation for why it can't be shifted around the way PPs usually can. Compare these three sentences:

> Jim arranged for us to be met at the airport.   [*for* = **For**$_{sbr}$]
> For us, Jim arranged to be met at the airport.   [*for* = **For**$_{prep}$]
> Jim arranged to be met at the airport for us.   [*for* = **For**$_{prep}$]

All three are grammatical, but their meanings are different. The first, with **For**$_{sbr}$, has Jim making arrangements under which someone will meet us at the airport. But in the other two, where *for* is the preposition **For**$_{prep}$, the claim made is that Jim got someone to meet him at the airport, yet in some way this benefited us (so we didn't have to do it).

Gerund-participial clauses

The gerund-participle is the verb form ending in *-ing*. It can occur as the verb of a clause either with a subject or without. And these clauses are unusual: they act almost as if they were NPs, so they often occur as the object of a preposition:

I'm worried about <u>going there after dark</u>.   [no subject]
I'm worried about <u>him going there after dark</u>.   [accusative subject]
I'm worried about <u>his going there after dark</u>.   [genitive pronoun subject]

In the first example, the gerund-participial clause has no subject of its own, so we pick up the obvious meaning from the main clause: the sentence means I'm worried about going there myself. But the other two mean that I'm worried about the safety of some other male person. And there is a choice about whether to say *him* or *his*. There's a mostly free choice between them. Never expect English to be neat and tidy. (Naturally there are purists who insist it should be tidy, so one of them must be an error; but I'll cover that later, in chapter 15.)

Past-participial clauses

There are two kinds of clause that need a principal verb in the past participle form. The first, and commonest, is the complement of the auxiliary ***Have***$_{aux}$, used to express what's known as the **perfect**:

The president has <u>given her a job in the White House</u>.
Have you <u>written that recommendation letter</u> yet?

This is an old-fashioned use of the term "perfect" that doesn't mean "without flaws"; it means "done with and completed."

It's for talking about actions completed in the past that have present relevance.

The past participle is also the form used for the principal verb in a passive clause:

Most of the plants in the field had been <u>trampled by wild hogs</u>.

These are often used as modifiers of nouns:

He produced a document <u>written in a foreign language</u>.

But passive clauses are a major and very important topic, and they deserve a chapter all to themselves. I'll turn to that now.

14

Passive clauses

Clear your mind of everything you've previously heard about what traditional books call the "passive voice." No aspect of English has been described more incompetently, or subjected to more invective in how-to-write books. What people say about the English passive clause is a confused jumble of inaccuracy and abuse. They call passives wordy, imprecise, and evasive; none of that is true. They often call the passive a "tense," but it has nothing to do with tense. And you can forget the term "voice" altogether; we won't be using it. (What is traditionally called "the passive voice" has nothing to do with anything vocal, or with what literary critics call authorial "voice.") There is a type of clause called the passive. The ones that aren't passive are referred to as active.

Above all, ignore suggestions that you should try to write without using passives. Nobody does. For everyone who writes normally, between about 10 and 20 percent of the clauses they write with verbs that take objects will be passive clauses. Sometimes a passive clause is exactly right for expressing what you want to say. Sometimes, in fact, it's obligatory. Far too many books treating passives simply say, "Use the active," and that's silly. Sometimes the active is the best choice, and sometimes the passive is; I'll explain why in what follows.

What are passive clauses?

First, let's make sure we can identify passives. Here's a very simple example of a clause with a verb that takes an object: *Burglars stole our TV.* That's an active clause. It has an alternative version that says the same thing in a different way: *Our TV was stolen by burglars.* That's a passive clause.

The active version has *burglars* as its subject NP. The passive version includes the reference to burglars, but not as the subject: it's at the end, in a PP beginning with *by*. I'll call that the **by-phrase** from now on.

Now, most PPs in English can be omitted, and the *by*-phrase of a passive is no exception. If you drop the *by*-phrase from our example you get *Our TV was stolen.* That's also a passive clause. But it hasn't got quite the same meaning, because it doesn't specify whether illegal entry into a building was involved.

I'll call a passive clause a **long passive** if it has a *by*-phrase and a **short passive** if it doesn't.

Now let's get a bit more precise. None of the traditional grammar books explain clearly what makes a clause passive, but it isn't too difficult. There are three defining properties:

1. The verb of a passive clause is always a **participle**. (The word *stolen* is the past participle of the verb **Steal**.)
2. In a passive clause, some NP that you would typically expect to find in a VP with that verb is either absent or located somewhere else. In active clauses the verb **Steal** will typically be followed by an object NP referring to the property that was illicitly taken, but in the VP *stolen by burglars* that's not true.

3. The clause is understood in a way that reverses the direction of the relation that the verb usually expresses. **Steal** typically talks about a relation between thief and property, but *was stolen by* talks about a relation between property and thief.

The NP that's omitted from the VP in a passive clause is often the one that would be the direct object in the active version (*our TV* is the direct object in *Burglars stole our TV*). But it can be the indirect object instead. In *They awarded Dylan a Nobel Prize*, the NP *Dylan* is the indirect object, and in the passive clause *Dylan was <u>awarded a Nobel Prize</u>* you can see that *Dylan* is missing from the underlined part. The verb *awarded* is missing its indirect object, the one that denotes the recipient or beneficiary.

The missing NP can also be the complement of a preposition, leaving the preposition stranded on its own. In these examples, the VP that makes the clause a passive (with its *by*-phrase in parentheses) is underlined:

We're going to be <u>laughed at</u> (<u>by our competitors</u>).
I've heard his financial affairs are being <u>looked into</u> (<u>by the auditors</u>).
I don't want my stuff <u>messed with</u> (<u>by anyone</u>) while I'm out.

Sentences of this sort, which can be either long or short passives, are relatively informal in style (as sentences with stranded prepositions often are), but they're fully grammatical.

The flipping of the relation in the meaning works in exactly the same way: *laugh at* talks about a relation between a person and something risible; *laughed at by* is about a relation between something risible and the amused people.

In many passive clauses, the past participle is preceded by a form of **Be**. This unfortunately leads haters of the passive to jump on all sentences with forms of **Be**, accusing them of being passives even when they're not. I've seen writing tutors accuse clauses like *She was beautiful* of being passives. However, a passive clause does not always follow a *Be* verb form. There are other verbs that can be followed by passive VPs. Here are some other examples of long passives, with the crucial passive VP underlined, and only the first three have *Be*:

ACTIVE	LONG PASSIVE
The Nazis committed many crimes.	*Many crimes were <u>committed by the Nazis</u>.*
Europeans never colonized Ethiopia.	*Ethiopia was never <u>colonized by Europeans</u>.*
His colleagues were laughing at him.	*He was being <u>laughed at by his colleagues</u>.*
I had a jeweler make this for me.	*I had this <u>made for me by a jeweler</u>.*
Last night the LAPD arrested Sally.	*Last night Sally got <u>arrested by the police</u>..*
We saw the police take Sally away.	*We saw Sally <u>taken away by the police</u>.*

It's also possible for passive VPs to have no immediately preceding verb. They can be (and often are) modifiers of nouns, as with the underlined phrases in these examples:

> *The president sits at a desk <u>made out of oak from the ship HMS Resolute</u>.*
> *People <u>bitten by a vampire</u> turn into vampires themselves when they die.*

The long passive

Long passives present information in a different way from their active rough equivalents: they express what's being said from a different perspective. An active clause like *Sue Grafton wrote the Alphabet Mysteries* is intuitively about Sue Grafton, and would be ideal for telling someone what she's famous for – creating the famous series of murder mystery novels that ran from *"A" Is for Alibi* to *"Y" Is for Yesterday*. The long passive version is *The Alphabet Mysteries were written by Sue Grafton*, and although it expresses the same fact, it presents it differently: we're now reading a fact about the book series. The passive would be appropriate for enlightening someone who wrongly thought that Patricia Cornwell wrote the Alphabet Mysteries.

It's not that one is good and the other bad. They present things in a different form and fit different contexts. An expert speaker or writer of English needs to know which one to use, and when.

Long passives are perfect for putting the spotlight on the person responsible for an act. They save up the information about who the culprit was until the end, where it can get some emphatic stress and be followed by a bit of a pause:

> *What this means, ladies and gentlemen, is that the murder must have been committed by ONE OF THE PEOPLE IN THIS ROOM!*

Another crucial fact about long passives that none of the traditional grammar books ever mention concerns their relation to the context. Long passives only really sound right if the NP following *by* is newly presented information – at least as new as what is conveyed by the subject of the clause. This has all sorts of consequences for what sounds right and what doesn't. Compare these examples:

> *Verdi was a composer and he wrote many operas.*
> *?? Verdi was a composer and many operas were written by him.*

Why does the second sentence sound so feeble and inept? It's not because weakness or ineptness are intrinsic to passives. It's because the *by*-phrase introduces nothing more than a second reference to Verdi, who was already mentioned in the first part and so isn't being newly introduced. A pronoun referring back to an earlier NP (like *him*) will hardly ever sound right in a *by*-phrase. But compare that sentence with this one:

> *Puccini wrote Tosca, yes, but Rigoletto was written by Verdi.*

This, with a passive in the second half, is exactly the way to put things when answering someone who thought Puccini wrote *Rigoletto*. It sounds better than the version with an active clause in the second half (which would be: *Puccini wrote Tosca, but Verdi wrote Rigoletto*). That's because *Verdi* is newly introduced information – the main information being presented, in fact. It's an ideal candidate for being put into the *by*-phrase of a passive.

Pronouns are the opposite of the ideal way to proffer new information. And since every utterance has an utterer and an intended addressee, so 1st- and 2nd-person pronouns are hardly ever new information. It would sound so utterly stupid for me to announce a major piece of good luck by saying *?The lottery has been won by me*. The bit about the lottery win is the hot new information, not the reference to myself. Putting the 1st-person pronoun *me* at the end by using a long passive is completely at odds with the newer-information condition on *by*-phrases.

For the same reason, we would say *Have you won the lottery?* rather than *?Has the lottery been won by you?* – a reference to you, the addressee, won't be new information, except perhaps in some fairly unusual context. (You might be able to think one up.)

There's another way in which passive clauses can sound weird or even false, despite being properly put together. This pair illustrates it:

> *Lee Child writes thrillers.*
> *?Thrillers are written by Lee Child.*

What's gone wrong here? Why does the passive in the second sentence seem the wrong way to put things? The answer is that by choosing the subject of a clause you will often be setting up the topic of a sentence by naming what you're talking about. If you're saying something about Lee Child, then "writes thrillers" is an important fact to provide about him – it's what he did for a living continuously between 1997 and 2022, and jointly with his brother after that. But if your topic is thrillers, then "written by Lee Child" is a very strange property to mention, because most thrillers don't have that property: there are tens of thousands of them, and only two or three dozen were written by Lee Child. So the trouble here is not about using the passive, it's about setting the topic.

One very striking point against the view that passives are bad in general is that a few verbs have to be used in the passive – the active version is ungrammatical:

UNGRAMMATICAL ACTIVE	GRAMMATICAL PASSIVE
People repute her to be very rich.	*She is <u>reputed to be very rich</u>.*
Many people say Bob to be lucky.	*Bob is <u>said by many people to be lucky</u>.*

Let me add two cautions here. First, beware of thinking that passives (or subjects) can be DEFINED by reference to what the clause is about. That won't work. It's true that *Mozambique was colonized by Portugal* seems to be about an African country, while *Portugal colonized Mozambique* seems to be about a European country. But we can use an NP as the subject in a passive clause even if it has no meaning at all, as with *it* in these examples:

Most of us believed it to be snowing.
It was <u>believed to be snowing by most of us</u>.

The underlined part of the second sentence is a passive VP, as its form shows (the past participle, the *by*-phrase, the lack of an object following *believe*); but the second sentence isn't SAYING SOMETHING ABOUT the meaningless *it*. And second, don't make the mistake of thinking that a subject NP always identifies the doer of an action or that an object NP always denotes something affected by some act; the same examples show that isn't always true either.

The short passive

Short passives are useful for a completely different reason from long passives. You can't leave the subject out of an independent clause in normal written English. In very casual colloquial utterances like *Beats me!*, people drop the subject, but not in writing. However, you can nearly always leave out PPs in the VP, including *by*-phrases. So in a passive clause it's possible to leave out mention of the agent or doer altogether. This can be extremely useful, and often makes the short passive exactly the right kind of clause to use. Short passives are perfect for saying what happened in cases where something was done by a person or persons whose identity is unknown or irrelevant:

SHORT PASSIVE	POSSIBLE *BY*-PHRASE NP
She was never seen again.	(anyone)
The house is believed to be haunted.	(people who believe in ghosts)
These are made in China.	(unknown factory workers)
Rumors were spread on Twitter.	(unknown rumor-mongers)
Somehow I got infected with Covid-19.	(some unidentified sick person)
The universe was created 13.8 billion years ago.	(unknown cosmic forces? God?)

Often it's not really clear what active clause could possibly express exactly the right sense. It might depend on how religious or superstitious you are. In the cases above, the passive versions are just what you want, because they leave the agent undetermined.

Yet writers on grammar and style attack the short passive as if it were a venomous snake. They call it evasive or dishonest because it conceals the identity of the doer. They love to cite politicians' slippery admissions that "Mistakes were made." But that slipperiness has nothing to do with passive clauses! There are all sorts of ways of avoiding a direct admission of liability. You can say *Mistakes occurred*, which is an active clause with a verb that doesn't take an object.

Warning budding writers off using short passives altogether is overkill. A short passive could allow an evasive statement that should have identified an agent, but often it doesn't do anything dishonest at all.

Advice for your own writing

Here's some more sensible advice than you'll find in most sources. Simply ignore those who say you should never use passives; that's stupid advice. The maximum number of additional words in a passive compared to its active equivalent is two, so the allegation that passives are "wordy" is false; in fact sometimes (when the alternative to a short passive involves inventing a subject to include) a passive will come out shorter than an active.

If you're writing for a teacher or boss who is irrationally hostile to passives, so you must obey, use the description in this chapter to make sure you know how to spot passives and carefully rephrase them. Otherwise, when you have no such malign oppressor, use passives just like every other writer does.

But use them carefully, judiciously, and gracefully. When writing a long passive, what you put in the *by*-phrase should be new information in the context. When writing a short passive, make sure you have good reasons for not supplying the identity of the doer. Don't be pointlessly evasive about agency. Use passives when they fit the context nicely – and don't use them when they don't.

As an exercise, try counting how many you've used. If between 10 and 20 percent of the verbs that can take objects are in passive clauses, that's comparable to the practice of most expert writers.

15

Relative clauses

A **relative clause** is a special kind of clause used mainly as a modifier of a noun. There are two crucially different ways in which a relative clause can belong to a sentence: **integrated** relatives are an integrated part of the structure and **supplementary** ones are loosely attached optional add-ons. I'll illustrate each in turn. In each one, you'll see that the relative clause has a meaning that in some rather vague sense modifies something occurring earlier, and that inside the relative clause there is always a kind of gap somewhere – a place where there would ordinarily have been some NP or PP but it's gone missing.

Integrated relative clauses

Integrated relative clauses are crucial parts of the structures of their sentences, and couldn't be left out without grossly changing the structure and the meaning, often making the sentence completely vacuous. (Other books call them "restrictive" or "defining" relatives – terms I don't use, because the clauses in question don't always restrict and don't always define.) The most important thing to remember about them is that in writing they are not flanked by commas. Here's an example, with the integrated relative clause in square brackets:

This is the package [*that I've been waiting for ___*].

The relative clause, *that I've been waiting for ___*, begins with the subordinator *That*_{sbr}. The meaning of the clause is roughly the same as *I've been waiting for this*, and it contributes essential information about the package. Instead of the NP you would expect after *for*, there is just a gap, marked by "___":

Some relative clauses begin with *wh*-pronouns, like this one, from Mario Puzo's novel *The Godfather*:

Mr. Corleone is a man [*who ___ likes to hear bad news immediately*].

Here the integrated relative clause is *who likes to hear bad news immediately*, which begins with the special relative pronoun *who*, and has roughly the same meaning as "he likes to hear bad news immediately". It modifies *man*, telling us what sort of man Mr. Corleone is. The clause is an absolutely crucial, integrated part of the message: without it, you have the stupidly empty statement: *Mr. Corleone is a man*.

A third example:

Nobody knows the trouble [*I've seen ___*].

In this one, the relative clause *I've seen* begins with neither a subordinator nor a relative pronoun. It's just the clause *I've seen it* with the direct object *it* left out. The relative clause modifies the noun *trouble*, and identifies what trouble the utterer is talking about.

Supplementary relative clauses

Supplementary relative clauses (which other books call "appositive relatives" or "non-restrictive relatives") are optional parenthetical interruptions of sentences. They can always be left out without changing the main assertion (though the ancillary information they contribute will be gone). The most important thing to remember about them in writing is that they must be separated off by punctuation, typically commas:

> *The duke, [who the organizers had hoped __ would present the award], was unable to attend owing to illness.*

The relative clause here means *the organizers had hoped he would present the award*, "he" being the duke. Normally there would have been a subject for *would present the award*, but here there is just a gap where an NP would have been. The main message of the whole sentence is that the duke was unable to attend. You could leave the supplementary relative clause out, and that message would still be conveyed: *The duke was unable to attend.* The sentence would not explain what the duke's role was going to be, but that's secondary to the main point about non-attendance.

Another example, differing in what kind of gap the relative clause has:

> *I'd now like to welcome Mr. Charles Bruntley, [to whom we are all profoundly grateful __].*

Here the gap "__" marks where a PP would have been; the relative clause means *we are all profoundly grateful to him* (where "him" means Mr. Bruntley). But saying *I'd now like to welcome Mr. Charles Bruntley*, on its own, would have done the job of introducing him. Mentioning the gratitude was just a non-obligatory aside.

And a third example, with a relative clause that is not associated with an NP:

The police station was only two minutes away, [which was very lucky].

Here the relative pronoun *which* refers back not to *police station* or *minutes* but to the fact that the police station was only two minutes away. That fact is what is being described as a piece of luck. But the good luck isn't the main point; it's supplementary. The central point is about how close the police station was.

Myths about relative clauses

Several myths about relative clauses have become established in the last century or two. One is the silly but widespread belief, invented by 19th-century British grammarians, that an integrated relative modifying a non-human noun should never begin with *which*, and another is that an integrated relative modifying a human noun should never begin with *that*. Here are the facts:

- Integrated relatives modifying human nouns mostly begin with Who_{rel}, as in *the girl who was responsible* or *the boy whose mother failed to collect him*. They also sometimes begin with *that*, as in *a person that we can trust*; this is less common, but it's not wrong.
- Integrated relatives modifying non-human nouns can begin with either *that* (as in *a date that works for everyone*) or *which* (as in *a date which will live in infamy*, from the speech by Franklin Roosevelt after Pearl Harbor was attacked). Neither is a mistake.
- Supplementary relatives modifying human nouns must

begin with *who*: we write *Queen Elizabeth II, who reigned for longer than any other monarch in history.*

• Supplementary relatives not associated with a human-referring noun must begin with *which*, as in *New York, which is perhaps the world's most important financial center.* (A hundred years ago, supplementary relatives sometimes had *that*, but it's now extraordinarily rare, and best regarded as an error.)

American copy editors insist on changing *which* to *that* in integrated relatives, because they believe that *which* should be limited to supplementary relatives. It seems impossible to talk them out of this belief (I have tried). It originates in an idea popularized by Henry and Frank Fowler in a 1906 book called *The King's English.* They noticed the extreme rarity of *that* introducing supplementary relatives, and it gave them an idea for tidying up: they decided English would be much neater if supplementary relatives always had *which*, and integrated relatives never did. Then the two would never overlap! Cool idea?

No. The problem is that *which* has always been common in integrated relatives, so the reform proposal they wanted to push was quixotic. It largely failed, because in writing that hasn't been altered by an American copy editor, *that* and *which* are very roughly level-pegging in integrated relatives.

Here's a nice example of a sentence about reporting wrong-doers in which choosing *that* instead of *which* happed to be a disaster for intelligibility:

> *IEEE has a way to denounce someone that protects the whistle-blower.*

This is grammatical but ambiguous: it could be talking about a method for denouncing the protector of a whistle-blower, or it could be talking about a way of denouncing people that provides protection for the whistle-blower. The sentence should have been written like this (violating the Fowler brothers' pseudo-rule):

> *IEEE has a way to denounce someone which protects the whistle-blower.*

That makes it clear (because of non-human-referring *which* rather than human-referring *who*) that the relative clause modifies the method of denouncing. The Institute of Electrical and Electronics Engineers is not offering a way to denounce someone who protects whistle-blowers. You can see that because the relative word *which* is not compatible with *someone*. The version with *that* obeys the Fowlers' rule, but is clearly the wrong choice: because it doesn't have a relative pronoun, it can't use the *who/which* distinction to make clear whether we're talking about a person or not.

The Fowler brothers were not dumb: they could see that their rule had all sorts of problems. In particular, it has many exceptions. Consider what happens in *the town in which they lived*. It has to have *which*, because ~~the town in that they lived~~ is not grammatical. Or consider a relative clause modifying the demonstrative word *That*$_{det}$: a phrase such as *that which remains* is clearly better than *??that that remains*.

But the Fowlers pushed their idea anyway, and unfortunately generations of teachers began to teach it, and today's copy editors learned from those teachers. It's a sad story.

I've explained all this so that you will know what's going on when you find some American editor or writing tutor has objected to your *which* and replaced it with *that*. You may find it is simplest to tolerate this monkeying with your prose. But don't let the tamperers tell you that they are correcting a mistake, because they aren't; they're implementing obedience to an unmotivated reform effort in late 19th-century England.

Fused relative clauses

There's another kind of relative clause, rather like an integrated relative, in which the modified noun and the relative pronoun have been fused together in a single word, usually the word *what*. The underlined part of this sentence is an example of it:

> *What Frankenstein created on that fateful night* would later ruin his life.

The meaning of the NP *what Frankenstein created that fateful night* is the same as if we had written an NP like *the thing* or *the creature* followed by *that* or the relative pronoun *which* but they had all been fused into the single word *what*.

It is important that an open interrogative content clause (an "indirect question" in traditional terms) may look exactly the same as a fused relative if it has *what* at the beginning. But there are simple tests to determine which is which. Take this example:

> *What Frankenstein created on that fateful night* doesn't matter.

In that sentence, the underlined words are the same ones, but they form an interrogative content clause; the whole sentence means that the answer to the question "What did Frankenstein create on that fateful night?" is not important.

One very simple test to see whether you have a fused relative or an open interrogative is to add the word *else* after *what*. It only fits with an interrogative *what*, so if you put it into a fused relative it ruins the grammaticality:

> *What else Frankenstein created on that fateful night doesn't matter.*
> ~~*What else Frankenstein created on that fateful night would later murder his fiancée.*~~

We can perform the same experiment with *what she's doing*. In *I don't know what she's doing* we have an interrogative content clause (it means "I don't know the answer to the question 'What is she doing?'"), and in *I don't like what she's doing* we have a fused relative (it means "I don't like the thing that she's doing"). And you can distinguish them with the *else* test:

I don't know what else she's doing.
~~I don't like what else she's doing.~~

16

Mythical grammar errors

There are hundreds of books on the market and pages on the web that will tell you that you are making grammatical errors. But if you can read any of this book you already have subconscious knowledge of a vast amount of grammar. You put hundreds of sentences together in conversation even on the quietest of days, and read or hear and understand hundreds or thousands more. You couldn't do all this if you didn't know a vast amount of English grammar. Most of what anyone needs to know about how to build sentences has got to be stuff you already know.

Yet you may still worry about committing blunders; you may worry that some unnoticed error will disadvantage you or make people think you're uneducated. This chapter is aimed at stemming that fear rather than stoking it. The truth is that the grammar know-it-alls are frequently grumbling about silly stuff. Some of the things they agonize over have been known for a century or more to be based on nothing but myths. And it won't take a lot of effort for you to learn which they are.

My plan is to begin by explaining in each of a few selected trouble spots what's correct and what's not, and then explain what the conservative usage advisers think the facts are, and finally tell you what you should actually do to avoid the slings and arrows of outrageous quibblers. I'll cover these topics:

* The so-called "split infinitive" (*to boldly go*).
* Subjects of gerund-participles (*him feeling bad*).
* Forms of coordinate pronouns (*to Jim and I*).
* **Who** and its inflected forms (*who they called*).
* *Like* with a clause complement (*like it used to be*).
* *less* vs. *fewer* (*less than eight of them*).
* *Different* prepositions (*different from/to/than*).
* Moral panic over modal adjuncts (*hopefully that won't happen*).
* Clause-initial connective adjuncts (*however* and *but*).
* The singular pronoun **They**$_{sg}$ (*someone might injure themself*).
* Mismatched coordinates (*both to A and B*).
* Stranding prepositions (*what they were looking at*).

The misnamed "split infinitive"

The superstition that modifiers (such as adverbs) mustn't be positioned between the *to* and the plain form verb in a *to*-infinitival is more than two centuries old: John Comly, in a grammar published in 1803, stated as his Rule 26 that "An adverb should not be placed between the verb of the infinitive mood and the preposition *to* which governs it." He didn't say why; he just put his foot down. And by the end of the 19th century many other grammarians thought they should stipulate something similar, and someone had coined the term "split infinitive" (which is a misnomer, because English doesn't have an "infinitive" verb form the way French and Latin do; no word is being split when you say *to finally leave*).

It was an odd rule to invent, because it bans a usage that was quite common by the 19th century, and has remained so ever since. A modifier of a verb is often much better placed just before that verb than anywhere else. Take a sentence like this one:

It would be sensible to at least consider revising the contract terms.

Here the modifying PP *at least* is positioned just before the verb it modifies, the verb *consider*. That's exactly the right position for it: the sentence is saying that what would be sensible is at least considering revision, possibly more than just considering it. Putting the modifier earlier (*It would be sensible at least to consider. . .*) sounds as if you mean sensible at least, possibly more than just sensible. Shifting it to later, after *consider* (*. . . to consider at least revising. . .*), sounds as if you mean at least revising it, possibly more than just revising. Moving it further in the same direction, to follow *revising* (*. . . to consider revising at least the contract terms*) or pushing it to the end of the VP (*. . . revising the contract terms at least*), makes it sound as if you mean at least the contract terms, possibly more than just those. Wrong meanings every time. The absolute best place for the modifying PP *at least* is between *to* and *consider*.

John Comly was parting company with the unconscious habits of expert writers when he stated his prohibition, and for some unknown reason many people made the mistake of believing him, instead of trusting themselves and each other. Don't follow them; trust the Associated Press style handbook, which in 2019, at long last, accepted that you can put modifiers between *to* and a verb. So I'm not advising you to boldly go where no writer has gone before.

Subjects with gerund-participles

In a clause where the main verb ends in *ing* (that is, in a gerund-participial clause), the subject may be in the genitive, or it may be in the accusative (if it's a pronoun) or the plain form (for an ordinary noun):

They didn't approve of <u>him</u> doing that.	[accusative]
They didn't approve of <u>his</u> doing that.	[genitive]
They didn't approve of <u>Jim</u> doing that.	[plain]
They didn't approve of <u>Jim's</u> doing that.	[genitive]

Both possibilities are found in respectable published prose, regardless of whether the subject is a pronoun or a full NP.

In the 18th and 19th centuries, some grammarians said that the genitive version was wrong and others said the opposite. What came to be the usual view in the 20th century was that only the genitive version was correct, and some conservative usage books today still say that. But they're wrong: it's very clear that both have been used by good writers for centuries, so forget the qualms of the nitpickers.

Sometimes using the genitive is definitely a mistake. For example, putting the genitive marker on a full NP that ends in a pronoun sounds truly dreadful:

~~It's ludicrous to imagine *a painting of him's* hanging in a museum.~~

Also note that there is a style difference: using the genitive usually sounds a bit more formal than using the accusative or plain form. That might be an advantage in some styles of writing. But most of the time either will do; don't agonize about the choice.

Forms of coordinate pronouns

One thing the grammar mavens really watch for is utterances in which a nominative pronoun is used where the accusative would be normal. This seems to happen most commonly with the lexeme *I* when it is just one part of a coordination formed with *and*: people say (and write) things like *This was news to Jim and I*. It drives the purists nuts. They howl about ignorant and illiterate clods defiling the sacred language of Shakespeare. It should be *to Jim and me*, they scream.

Yet Shakespeare himself used the nominative like this. In a scene in *The Merchant of Venice*, Bassanio reads aloud to Portia a letter from his friend Antonio, to whom he owes money. Antonio has borrowed money from the Jewish merchant Shylock, and cannot repay it, so Shylock is demanding a pound of Antonio's flesh as the promised collateral. Antonio writes:

> *Sweet Bassanio, my ships have all miscarried, my creditors grow cruel, my estate is very low, my bond to the Jew is forfeit; and since in paying it, it is impossible I should live, all debts are cleared* <u>*between you and I,*</u> *if I might but see you at my death.*

It's a bit eccentric to revere Shakespeare but revile *between you and I*.

The purists commonly imply that they're dealing with speakers so dumb that they confuse *I* with *me*. But that's just not true: nobody is confused enough to say ~~Me love you~~ when they mean *I love you*; no one mistakenly says ~~Don't hurt I~~ for *Don't hurt me*.

(All right, yes, Tarzan famously says "Me Tarzan," meaning "I am Tarzan," and there was an episode of *Star Trek* where an alien entity said "No hurt I." But give me a break: Tarzan was raised by apes, and the *Star Trek* alien was a kind of acid-spewing mobile rock. I'm talking about competent Standard English-speaking humans who were raised by humans, okay?)

The question in a nutshell is whether the rules about choosing nominative or accusative forms of pronouns apply when the pronoun is one of two or more NPs linked with a coordinator. The situation regarding what people actually say is amazingly confused; it really dents your confidence (if you had any) that the grammar of English is a fixed body of doctrine that all native English speakers tacitly know. Take these four potential utterances, three of which would be generally regarded as ungrammatical:

She and I went to the same school.
??Me and her went to the same school.
??Her and I went to the same school.
??She and me went to the same school.

The first is strict Standard English, and occurs much more often than the others. There's no question about whether it's the pattern you should use in serious writing. But I've actually heard all four patterns from native speakers of English, so expect variety in everyday speech. The form of pronouns in coordinations just seems to be something that people don't instinctively get right. In fact when the 1st-person singular pronoun *I* ends a coordination that follows a verb or preposition, many educated speakers seem to think the nominative sounds better than the accusative, so they say: *??This was news to Jim and I.* But this conflicts with what's generally regarded as standard: use the form that would have been correct if the pronoun had been used in that position on its own. Since you'd say *This was news to me*, you should write *This was news to Jim and me.* On this, there's every reason to grant the purists what they prefer. But don't expect to see universal agreement from others, and don't assume people who say *??to Jim and I* are stupid (remember Antonio's letter to Bassanio).

There are a couple of other cases where a pronoun is only part of an NP. First, there are two plural pronouns that are also used as determinatives. The first is **You**$_{pl}$ as in *It's time for* <u>*you children*</u> *to go to bed*, which raises no problems because it doesn't show a nominative/accusative difference, but the other one is **We**, where we do get a choice between the nominative and the accusative:

<u>*We older members*</u> *are not sure we want things to change.*
Does that apply to <u>*us undergraduates*</u> *as well?*

Again the rule is supposed to be that you're meant to put these personal determinatives in the case form that would be used if a pronoun occupied the position of the whole NP. But again, people don't always get it right! A quality newspaper in Australia published a letter containing the completely ungrammatical sentence ~~Are any of our politicians really listening to we quiet Australians?~~ without correcting it; and then just a few days later published a letter with the similarly ungrammatical sentence ~~Meanwhile, us fornicators, adulterers and drunkards are in for a roasting.~~ The first should have had *us* (paralleling *listening to us*), and the second should have had *we* (paralleling *We are in for a roasting*, not ~~Us are in for a roasting~~). So even people who are literate enough to write letters to a serious newspaper get confused.

One other situation where people differ concerns clauses with the verb omitted:

> *They were an odd couple, she neat and quiet, he restless and flamboyant.*
> *They were an odd couple, her neat and quiet, him restless and flamboyant.*

The second version, with accusative forms (*her* and *him*), is more informal, and sounds quite natural to me. Opinions will differ. But if you want a recommendation, I'd say go with the first version in serious writing.

The pronoun *Who* and its inflected forms

Two distinct lexemes share the word-forms *who* (nominative), *whom* (accusative), and *whose* (genitive): the interrogative pronoun that I'll call Who_{que} (where "que" suggests "question") and the relative pronoun I'll call Who_{rel} (where "rel" signals "relative"). The differences between them are quite sharp, and it is surprising that virtually no grammar books seem to have ever noticed these facts:

- *Who*~rel~ doesn't have an independent genitive. *Whose did they reject?* is fine (with the independent genitive of *Who*~que~), but you can't say ~~They accepted most submissions, though Jim, whose they rejected, was crushed~~ (with the independent genitive of *Who*~rel~).
- *Who*~que~ is strictly singular, as verb agreement shows: although you can say *How many people really care?*, you can't say ~~Who really care?~~
- Although both *Who*~que~ and *Who*~rel~ are used mostly to refer to humans, *Who*~que~ has a genitive form (*whose*) that can refer to non-humans, as in *I want you to repair all the chairs whose legs are loose*. With *Who*~que~, this isn't possible: a question like *Whose legs are loose?* can only be understood as asking about loose-legged humans, not chairs.

By the way, I simplified slightly by saying that *Who*~que~ is used for humans. In practice, that gets extended to other ethically person-like entities, such as pets (*the only dog who has ever really understood me*) or intelligent robots (*Marvin, the paranoid android, who was in a bad mood as usual*).

When we switch to talking about thoroughly non-human things, **What** and **Which** are both used in interrogatives (*What was that? Which one was it?*). In relatives, **Which** is used for non-humans (compare *the horse which won* with *the woman who won*), but **What** isn't.

The whom *problem*

The thorniest issues about both *Who*~que~ and *Who*~rel~ concern the accusative. The form *whom* has been very slowly slipping out of use for a long time. It generally strikes people as very formal, though it's by no means extinct even in conversational use. Its marginal status enables grammar snobs to ding people for failing to use it when they could have used it, or for using it when they shouldn't have. Here is a brief run-down of what you need to know (it's necessarily a bit tedious, but don't shoot the messenger).

The basic rule is supposed to be that you use *who* only when it's the subject of a tensed verb, and *whom* or *whose* elsewhere.

- When either **Who**$_{que}$ or **Who**$_{rel}$ begins a clause and it's not the subject of a tensed verb, the sticklers insist that it should have the form *whom*. So they claim it's a mistake to write *Who do you want to see?* or *The specialist who I originally wanted to see wasn't available,* where *who* is understood as the object of *see*. It's a bit crazy to call these mistakes, of course (and I refuse to mark them as ungrammatical): millions of English speakers say and write such sentences every day, and not through careless slips.

- In the case of spoken English, the frequency of clauses beginning with *whom* in ordinary conversation has pretty much collapsed to zero. *Whom* hardly ever occurs except after prepositions (*the specialist to whom I was referred*), and even there it sounds fairly stiff and formal; the normal way to say it would be *the specialist I was referred to*.

- Having been told that such uses of *who* are mistakes, people sometimes try too hard to avoid being caught using a *who* that should have been a *whom*, and end up choosing *whom* even when it's the subject of a tensed verb. A manager of my acquaintance told me that after some promotions had been denied he received a memo from his superiors including the sentence "It is strongly recommended that you meet with staff whom have been unsuccessful in order to provide support." The phrase ~~staff whom have been unsuccessful~~ is flamingly ungrammatical, but the writer in the upper administration seems to have thought that in a formal memo it was a sin to use the *who* form anywhere.

- Despite its formal character, and the way many people are losing their grip on how and where to use it, *whom* hasn't completely died out. Even in informal conversation, people often use the accusative of **Who**_{rel} after prepositions in relative clauses. People will say *The specialist to whom I was originally referred wasn't available* – though more frequently you'd hear *The specialist who I was originally referred to wasn't available.* (Of course, in a relative clause like this you can avoid using **Who**_{rel} altogether, by saying *the specialist that I was originally referred to* or *the specialist I was originally referred to.*)

One of the oddest things about *whom* is that there are sentence types where it is not clear even to experts whether you should use it or not. Which of these two examples would you regard as correct, and which is the mistake?

We're talking about someone who everybody agrees is qualified.
We're talking about someone whom everybody agrees is qualified.

I gave a rule for *who* earlier: use *who* when it's the subject of a tensed verb. But you should now be able to see that the rule isn't phrased carefully enough. In the two cases above, *who(m)* is the subject of the *is* clause (as in *Who is qualified?*), but not the subject of the *agrees* clause (which has *everybody* as its subject). Which is relevant? We need a clearer guide.

Delving into English literature, we find (to our horror, perhaps) that examples of both sorts have appeared in all kinds of excellent English writing for centuries. Shakespeare actually used both. The one that the grammar purists generally like best is the one with the nominative *who*, but you find sentences in Shakespeare like "Young Ferdinand, whom they suppose is drowned" (that's in *The Tempest*). Yet Shakespeare also referred to Brutus and Cassius "who, you all know, are honourable men". The Bard of Avon isn't going to settle this.

The bottom line is that confusion over *who* and *whom* is completely understandable; the factual situation is extraordinarily confusing – it almost seems malign. My advice to you will be deliberately simple (you might even say simplistic):

- Never use *whom* immediately before the tensed verb of its clause: ~~Whom is interested in this?~~ is decisively ungrammatical.
- When writing, always use *whom* after a preposition that it belongs with: *the writer to whom it was awarded* is normal, and ~~the writer to who it was awarded~~ is not. (Colloquially, people say things like *They gave it to who?* with *who* as object of a verb, but that's definitely informal.)
- In those tricky cases like *someone who(m) everyone agrees is qualified*, where looking at literature doesn't definitely settle the matter, you might as well use *who*. I say this for three reasons: (i) some purists insist it's the only correct form, and there's no profit in getting up their nose; (ii) *who* is more frequent anyway; and (iii) *who* never sounds pompous; so it's win-win-win.

Like with a clause complement

An ancient tradition among conservative nitpickers says that the preposition *like* shouldn't take a tensed clause as its complement. *Like* allows a gerund-participial clause, of course, because all prepositions do: *like falling off a log* is grammatically perfect for everyone. The controversy is about *like he had fallen off a log*.

Two different kinds of tensed clause occur as complements of *like* in Standard English prose: content clauses (which are full clauses with no missing bits) and comparative clauses (which have a missing constituent). But both are informal in style. Here are some examples of *like* with a content clause:

He just walked in and took over <u>like he owned the whole world</u>.
My girlfriend was looking at me <u>like she wanted to kill me</u>.
Most of the album sounds <u>like he was drunk when he recorded it</u>.

For these, the nitpickers would replace *like* by *as if*. But the version with *like* is not a mistake; rather it's casual.

And here are some examples of *like* with a comparative clause (using "[__]" to show where the missing bit would have been):

I just don't see this like other people do [__].
You can buy Narcan over the counter, like anyone can [__] these days.
Winston tastes good like a cigarette should [__].

There was a media brouhaha when the William Esty advertising agency devised that last sentence as a slogan to advertise Winston cigarettes in 1954. The celebrated news presenter Walter Cronkite was told to utter the slogan as part of acknowledging the sponsors of *The Morning Show*, and he refused, because it violated what he thought was a grammatical rule. An announcer's voice-over had to be used for that endorsement.

Of course, the shock and revulsion was all a bit overdone. A kind of grammatical virtue signaling. It probably did great things for Winston's advertising visibility. Sentences of this sort are fully grammatical, but they are informal. Cronkite was just insisting that he would only use formal style when on camera. It was like that in the old days.

You can turn the above examples into formal style in various ways:

I don't see this <u>in the same way that</u> other people do.
You can buy this over the counter, <u>as</u> anyone can these days.
Winston tastes good, <u>the way</u> a cigarette should.

So make replacements of that sort if you're concerned about whether people regard your writing as too informal and chatty. But if you're writing a novel it would be silly to think you couldn't use *like* with a tensed clause complement.

Less vs. *fewer*

Grammar sticklers go into hissy fits at sentences like *There were less people at the reception than I expected.* They may even blanch at *The conference attracted less than 50 people.* What they're concerned about is that the determinative *less* is the one to use when talking about quantities of stuff, as in *less money* or *less fuel.* Since people can be counted, they say, it must be *fewer people at the reception* and *fewer than 50 people.* Confusing the two, they insist, is wrong.

This is a classic grammatical problem area, and (trigger warning) it's quite a complicated one. Take a deep breath, and I'll begin.

To start with, the purists are being unjust: people do NOT confuse *less* with *fewer.* Nobody ever says *He earns fewer money now* or *My new hybrid uses fewer fuel.* People know the difference! They know that *fewer* can only be used with count nouns.

What's going on is that *less* has been broadening its use and encroaching on part of the territory of *fewer.* For centuries, *less* was used in at least some contexts with count nouns, but in 1770 a scholar named Robert Baker tried to put a stop to that, claiming that *fewer* might be "more elegant" and "more strictly proper." Somehow, over the following two hundred years, usage authorities began to think Baker's preference was an inviolable rule. It isn't, and never was. Absolutely everyone seems to agree that it is fine to say *He has been with the company for less than five years,* and *year* is a count noun, so the generalization offered by the sticklers is wrong.

You have to use your common sense here. Manuela Hoelterhoff once wrote in a *Wall Street Journal* opera review the following statement about mezzo-soprano Tatiana Troyanos:

> *I suspect her martial aria would glitter as much with a few less embellishments.*

And she was right, because that's obviously better than writing *?a few fewer embellishments.*

What's true is that, in general, *less* followed by a plural count noun (*?less apples*) is uncommon, and *fewer* is normally preferred.

Perhaps the nastiest wrinkle here is that there are nouns that used to be irregular plurals of count nouns (usually from Latin) but are shifting to become mass nouns. The classic example is *data.* Older scientists who know some Latin think of it as the plural of the count noun *datum* (which means "a thing that is given"), so they would write *The data are not sufficiently numerous to establish the hypothesis.* What's much more common today (in a world where the phrase "big data" has become familiar) is to think of quantities of information as a mass of stuff, like sand on a beach, and to say things like *The data is flooding in now we have the new machine.*

Simple cases like *We need more data* are compatible with either: notice, you can say either *more pebbles*, with the plural of a count noun, or *more sand*, using the singular of a mass noun.

Crucially, though, some determinatives are compatible only with one or the other: *many* is compatible only with count nouns (*many pebbles*, which takes plural agreement, but not ~~*many sand*~~); but *much* is compatible only with mass nouns (*much sand*, which takes singular agreement, but not ~~*much pebbles*~~).

Keep in mind that *few* works grammatically like *many*, and *little* works like *much.* Here is a beautiful real-life example, a totally ungrammatical sentence taken from the normally well-written news magazine *The Economist*, where a sub-editor got confused:

> *Even in Britain, where economic data reach farther back than in any other country, little reliable labour-force data exist until the mid-1800s.*

The first occurrence of *data* shows us that *The Economist* takes the conservative view, treating *data* as a plural, so it uses plural agreement (as in *they reach* rather than *it reaches*). But then comes the second occurrence, *little reliable labour-force data*. It has the determinative *little*, which only goes with mass nouns. If *data* is a mass noun, it should take singular agreement: *little reliable labour-force data exists.* (Ignore the fact that *little* has another life as a size adjective; that's just a distractor here. The sense of *little* in *little pebbles* is irrelevant; *little data* doesn't mean data of diminutive size, it means not much data!)

It looks as if a sub-editor spotted the sequence *data exists* and changed it to *data exist* in keeping with house style, but failed to notice the consequence of the determinative *little*. This created a grammatical error: *little reliable labour-force data exist* is every bit as ungrammatical as *little wine were left in the bottle*.

Notice, I'm not telling you whether to be conservative the way *The Economist* tries to be, treating *data* as a plural count noun, or whether to treat it as a singular mass noun the way modern scientists do when they talk about having "not much data." You can decide for yourself. But once you've decided, you have to be careful to stick to your decision and make sure the verbs agree correctly!

Different prepositions

Is chalk different *to* cheese, or different *from* cheese, or different *than* cheese? All three have been used often enough, so don't imagine that your use of one or another might reveal ignorance. It won't.

But if you'd like to be in step with contemporary American English, it looks as if *different from* is now overwhelmingly the most frequent. *Different to* does occur, more so in British English. And although *different than* occurs moderately often, *different from* is much more common. So if you're anxious or in doubt, write *different from*.

With the adverb *differently, from* is very common (*Women do things differently from men*), but *than* is obligatory when what follows is a comparative clause (*Bankers view capital differently than regulators do*).

Moral panic over modal adjuncts

At the end of the 1939 film *Gone With the Wind*, Scarlett O'Hara asks Rhett Butler where she will go and what she will do now that he has rejected her, and his famous reply was *Frankly, my dear, I don't give a damn*. He was using the adverb *frankly* not as a **manner adjunct** meaning "in a candid manner" (as in *Let me speak frankly*), but in a sentence-introducing role, meaning something like "What I'm going to say in this sentence is my candid opinion."

In an exactly parallel way, the adverb *hopefully* is a manner adjunct in *It's better to travel hopefully than to arrive* (where *hopefully* means "optimistically" or "with a heart full of hope"), but in a sentence like *Hopefully we all look in our rearview mirrors when we drive*, the same adverb isn't a manner adjunct (it's not that we look in our rearview mirrors with optimism);

instead it means something like "What I'm going to say in this sentence is my optimistic opinion."

Nobody had ever thought of grumbling about such a thing until the early 1960s, when after a bit of an upswing in the frequency of this second use of *hopefully* various members of the New York literati got it into their heads that there was something wrong with using *hopefully* like that. They wanted people to restrict it to the manner adjunct sense. Wilson Follett took up the cause, and his 1966 book *Modern American Usage* contained disapproving words about the modal adjunct use.

By 1972, E.B. White had picked up the idea and added a flailing, incoherent, angry, foaming-at-the-mouth paragraph to the 2nd (1972) edition of his revision of *The Elements of Style*. He calls the sentence-introducing *hopefully* silly, unclear, free-floating, offensive, ambiguous, soft, nonsense – in other words, he has no idea what he wants to say about it. He just hates it so much that he wants to spit.

There is no reason for this. Using adverbs as sentence-modifying introducers of this sort is completely standard. *CGEL* calls them **modal** adjuncts, because they modify the way the content of the clause relates to reality in the same way that modal auxiliaries do. Nobody objects when adverbs like *clearly* or *honestly* or *frankly* do the same thing, so all of these pairs of sentences are comparable:

They couldn't see the warning sign clearly.	[manner]
Clearly, they couldn't see the warning sign.	[modal]
I don't know how to earn a living honestly anymore.	[manner]
Honestly, I don't know how to earn a living anymore.	[modal]
I'm not ashamed to talk frankly about it.	[manner]
Frankly, I'm not ashamed to talk about it.	[modal]
She won't speak hopefully about the budget.	[manner]
Hopefully, she won't speak about the budget.	[modal]

All these adverbs had developed secondary uses as modal adjuncts at least a hundred years ago. The brouhaha over *hopefully* was pretty much over within twenty years. It should go without saying that *hopefully* was never barred from its older use as a manner adjunct meaning "in an optimistic spirit" (as in *As I cut up the meat, the dog watched me hopefully*); but the modal adjunct use is now much more frequent (check it out in your own reading). If anyone suggests that you shouldn't use *hopefully* as a modal adjunct, tell them not to be silly, and show them this book. Hopefully that'll shut them up.

Clause-initial connective adjuncts

However is an adverb that generally functions as a **connective adjunct**. (It can also be a modifier of adjectives, with a completely different meaning, as in *However careful you are, they will catch you*. Ignore that sense of the word.) When appearing at the beginning of a main clause, it links the sentence to what has gone before in a particular way, like this:

> *Most of the students left as soon as the class was over. However, one of them stayed behind.*

The *however* introduces a new piece of meaning and suggests it might be contrary to what you might have expected. *But* is a coordinator that does a very similar job semantically; you could write this, with almost exactly the same meaning:

> *Most of the students left as soon as the class was over. But one of them stayed behind.*

The meanings are basically the same, but there's a real difference in the grammar. A small point is that connective adjuncts often take a following comma but coordinators don't:

Most of the students left as soon as the class was over. ~~But, one of them stayed behind.~~

More important is the fact that because *but* is a coordinator it can link the two sentences to make a single coordinate sentence. *However* cannot do this:

Most of the students left when the class ended, but one of them stayed behind.
~~Most of the students left when the class ended, however one of them stayed behind.~~

A third difference is that *however*, like lots of other adverbs, can be placed after the subject, or after the first auxiliary verb, or at the end of the clause:

Most of the students left when the class ended. One of them, however, stayed behind.
Most of the students left when the class ended. One of them stayed behind, however.

If you attempt to do the same with *but*, you get screamingly ungrammatical results which no one would write:

~~Most of the students left when the class ended; one of them, but, stayed behind.~~
~~Most of the students left when the class ended; one of them stayed behind, but.~~

This is one distinction that it's important to get right. Punctuating as if *however* were just like *but* is a very common error in inexpert writing.

One additional note. There's a myth peddled by early 20th-century usage books that there's something wrong with putting *however* at the beginning of a sentence. This is twaddle, and you should ignore it. Excellent writers often begin sentences with *however*. It is true that a century ago different authors had strikingly different preferences, possibly indicating formality level: the ponderous novels of Henry James have sentences beginning with *"However,"* much less than the humorous writing of Mark Twain, so maybe in the early 1900s such a sentence opening was felt to be more informal; but today both positioning options are commonplace. Far too many "rules" foisted upon 21st-century students actually stem from opinions held long before the First World War. Don't let antiquated writing advice nudge you toward writing like your great-grandparents!

The singular pronoun *They*~sg~

There is a long tradition of usage books warning you that *they* is a plural pronoun and should never be used to refer back to grammatically singular NPs like *any student* or *everyone*. What lies behind this is the view of some 19th-century purists who were worried about illogicality. *Everyone* is grammatically singular, they noted (it originates as a collapsing of "every one"); we can see that it's singular by the form of the underlined verb in *Everyone has gone*. It's only the meaning that's plural: *Every pig likes acorns* has the same meaning as *All pigs like acorns*.

They, on the other hand, is plural, as we see from the underlined verb form in *They have had enough* (and also the meaning: *they* here has roughly the same meaning as "those people"). Therefore, the purists reasoned, mistakenly, it must be a logical error to say *Everyone says they have had enough*.

But why should anyone think that because *they* takes plural agreement it therefore cannot refer back to something that doesn't? There's nothing wrong with *The team enjoyed their beers*; surely nobody seriously thinks it would sound better to say *The team enjoyed its beers*.

The critics haven't thought it through, and haven't studied enough literature. Renowned and excellent writers have been using sentences in which *They* refers back to a singular NP for centuries:

> Nobody here seems to look into an author, ancient or modern, if they can avoid it.
> (Lord Byron, in a letter, 1805)

> I would have everybody marry if they can do it properly.
> (Jane Austen, in *Mansfield Park*, 1814)

> A person can't help their birth.
> (William Makepeace Thackeray, in *Vanity Fair*, 1848)

> when everyone has practically said whatever they had to say
> (Lady Bracknell, in Oscar Wilde's *The Importance of Being Earnest*, 1895)

> Somebody taught you, didn't they?
> (E.B. White, in *Charlotte's Web*, 1952)

> too hideous for anyone in their senses to buy
> (W.H. Auden, in an article, 1955)

You've got to be pretty arrogant to think you know more about writing correct English than Byron, Austen, Thackeray, Wilde, White, or Auden.

A more sensible idea would be that the purists who disapprove of singular *They* are a bunch of befuddled dimwits who should be ignored.

They has been common for centuries to refer back to grammatically singular NPs that don't refer to a specific known person: *Nobody ever thinks it should apply to them*; *A child who thinks they don't fit in at school in will be unhappy*; *Whoever left their keys in the washroom should come and collect them*. However, until the end of the 20th century it was never found with referential singular NPs like people's names, so *Chris says they left their wallet in the taxi* would not have been thought grammatical, but in the last twenty-five years or so there has been a fairly successful movement to persuade the news media to adopt such pronoun use when referring to people who identify as non-binary or gender-queer. So today when writing about non-binary people like the singer Sam Smith, journalists write *Sam Smith is recording new songs for their next album.* Older people will think that sounds very odd, and that is because back in the 20th century such sentences never occurred.

Mismatched coordinates

The first of these three examples, where I have underlined the coordinates, is unremarkable, but people often write sentences like the second and the third as well:

> *I was expected either <u>to accept this</u> or <u>to resign from the committee.</u>*
> *I was expected either <u>to accept this</u> or <u>resign from the committee.</u>*
> *I was expected to either <u>accept this</u> or <u>to resign from the committee.</u>*

I haven't struck out the second and third as ungrammatical, but many authorities would. In the first, the *either* comes at the beginning of a coordination that is balanced: each coordinate is a *to*-infinitival complement. In the second, the *either* is in a sense too early, so the first coordinate is a *to*-infinitival but the second is a bare infinitival. And in the third, the *either* comes too late: the first coordinate is a bare infinitival but the second is a *to*-infinitival.

The shifting may be in either direction, and occurs so commonly that you should probably regard it as an option in Standard English: we could say that speakers reposition *either* when the coordination has the coordinator *or*, and reposition *both* when the coordinator is *and*, and reposition *neither* when the coordinator is *nor*. However, style purists hate to see these shifted determinatives. It is easy to give them what they want by positioning these words in a way that makes the coordinates balanced. The important point is that if you look at what follows the *either* or *both* or *neither*, you ought to see a pair of phrases of the same type linked by a coordinator:

> We bought presents for both <u>our son</u> and <u>his boyfriend</u>.
> [NP & NP: *both* comes before an NP and so does *and*]
> We bought presents both <u>for our son</u> and <u>for his boyfriend</u>.
> [PP & PP: *both* comes before a PP and so does *and*]

Keep the coordinates balanced and keep the sticklers off your back; why annoy them when you don't have to and there's no gain in expressiveness or style?

Stranding prepositions

The dumbest myth in the whole history of the English language is the cockamamie notion that something might be wrong with having a sentence or a phrase with a preposition stranded at the end. We actually know who perpetrated this nonsense: John Dryden – a poet, translator, playwright, essayist, and literary critic – published an essay in 1672 defending his critical views on the work of his fellow writers, and observed sniffily that Ben Jonson (as famous as Shakespeare back then) had written a line ending in *from*, and commented that putting a "preposition in the end of the sentence" was "a common fault with him."

Why was it a "fault"? Dryden had nothing to say about that. And he admitted that he had noticed the same supposed "fault" in his own writings. (He started editing them out of later editions.)

But Dryden was so extraordinarily influential that his eccentric criticism stuck. To this day, there are teachers who believe that students should be taught not to use perfectly acceptable sentences like *No one knew what she was talking about.*

The issue actually has nothing to do with prepositions ending a sentence, or a clause. *What she was talking about wasn't obvious* has the same feature: a preposition that is NOT IMMEDIATELY FOLLOWED BY ITS OBJECT. Linguists call such prepositions **stranded**. Languages like French, Spanish, and German don't permit it. Languages like Norwegian, Icelandic, and English do.

Stranding is normal and very frequent in relative or open interrogative clauses, and some other kinds. The following examples have a blank "__" at the point in the sentence where an NP object would normally have been found, and I underline the phrase that we understand as being associated with that position, putting square brackets round the crucial part of the sentence:

[*Which restaurant* did you go to __] *for lunch?*
If they don't know [*what* the person died of __] *they do an autopsy.*
A person [*who* nobody connects with __] *is not a suitable candidate.*
[*What a ridiculous process* we had to go through __] *to get planning permission.*

It's astonishing that there are educated users of English who still think sentences like these are bad, and struggle to avoid them. But there are such people, especially in the USA.

In formal style, there's usually a way of avoiding stranding: you can put the preposition up front along with some word like *whom* or *which* that belongs with it. You could write *To whom was the letter addressed?* instead of *Who was the letter addressed to?*; but that's probably not a good idea, because it sounds so pompous. And in some cases you don't really have that option. Look at these examples of stranding:

They scarcely knew [*what they were looking at* __].
Machine learning is one subject [*I try to keep up with* __].
There's no cinema in the town [*that I come from* __].

Putting the preposition at the beginning of its clause in these cases would be a hopeless strategy: for the first two it makes them sound ridiculous (I've used the ?? prefix on those), and for the third it would be totally ungrammatical:

> ??*They scarcely knew at what they were looking*
> ??*Machine learning is a field with which I try to keep up.*
> ~~There's no cinema in the town from that I come.~~

So in these cases stranding is pretty much unavoidable. But people living in terror of grammatical sin will sometimes write (or even speak) hopelessly ungrammatical sentences as they struggle to avoid stranding. I once received an email containing the sentence ~~*I hope you will understand of what I am speaking*~~. The sender meant *I hope you'll understand what I'm talking about,* but seemed to think that wasn't fit to be typed.

Once when I got no results from a search on the website of *The New Yorker,* I saw the error message ??*I couldn't find that for which you were looking*! Hilarious. They apparently thought that *I couldn't find what you were looking for* would fall beneath the magazine's respectability standards. (They changed the error message a few weeks later after it was mocked online.)

In some examples, gaps follow prepositions but no *wh-*word like *who* or *which* is involved:

> [<u>*Behavior like that,*</u> *we will not put up with __ in this company.*]
> *If there's something* [*you're not happy with __*]*, you should say so.*
> [*An animal that you're afraid of __*] *isn't a suitable pet.*
> *I've got some pictures* [*for you to look at __*].

In these sentences you can't avoid stranding by putting the preposition earlier, because there's nothing to put it with. Yet they were never grammar mistakes, no matter how far back you go in the history of English. Dryden's idea that it was a "fault" to use normal English has no basis at all.

17

Spelling and punctuation

L et me make one thing clear: in this chapter I am doing no more than scratching the surface. On these topics, there are really excellent reference works available. All I'm going to do is make a few points that are often missed or not put clearly enough.

The English writing system

English has one of the worst alphabetic writing systems in the solar system, so let's not pretend otherwise. The spelling conventions are complex, chaotic, and riddled with exceptions. Some letters are used for a slew of different tasks and others aren't needed at all; some differently pronounced words are spelled the same; some differently spelled words are pronounced identically... The whole system is a disgrace. If the spelling rules for English had been established by a government, you'd vote them out.

But they weren't, of course: they just evolved over a thousand chaotic years, during which the ruling class was replaced a couple of times, and printing was invented, and the

Renaissance happened, and the British Commonwealth was founded, and the USA was born, and humans fought the most wasteful wars in history.

The traditional twenty-six letters of the alphabet and the other symbols you have to know (punctuation marks, currency symbols, foreign letters, and symbols like @ and &) are an ill-assorted bunch of varying utility, and the spelling system is chaos, but we're stuck with the system forever. You shouldn't despise yourself for sometimes making spelling mistakes, but life is not fair: you will be blamed anyway. Sad to say, people judge the intelligence and employability of other people by whether they can spell and punctuate correctly. So you simply have to work at learning spellings and punctuation conventions. There's no alternative.

American and British spelling

In case you are thinking that reform or regularization might someday lift or erase this burden, let me disappoint you some more: it won't happen. There will never be a thoroughly revised system of English spelling. Noah Webster's revisions, which created the American spelling system, were supposed to be a step in that direction, but they only made things more complicated by forcing us to worry about whether to use American spellings like *center, color, defense, dialog, fueling,* and *generalize,* or British ones like *centre, colour, defence, dialogue, fuelling,* and *generalise.* (The *-ize/-ise* distinction is not geographically aligned: *-ise* is the usual spelling in British sources, though the *Oxford English Dictionary* uses *-ize,* agreeing with most American writers and publishers. Neither can be called a spelling mistake. Your duty is simply to be consistent, and not confuse cases of the *-ize/-ise* Greek-derived suffix with words like *surprise* or *arise* that just happen to end in *ise.*)

This is one linguistic topic on which Wikipedia is wonderful: it has an excellent article headed "American and British English spelling differences."

Apostrophes

The apostrophe is a near-useless extra letter of the alphabet that serves no substantial purpose, and has the additional annoying property of having exactly the same shape as a completely different item which has an important function: the right single quotation mark.

The apostrophe has no grammatical or phonetic role. Unlike any other letter, it's NEVER associated with any sound of its own. Various letters are silent in certain words (like the *g* in *gnaw* or *sign*; the *e* in *horde*; the first letter in *hour*, *knot*, or *psycho*; and the *o* in my first name *Geoff*); but the thing about the apostrophe is that it is ALWAYS silent.

What's more, hardly any misunderstandings would result if it were scrapped. There's no difference between a writer's conference, a writers' conference, and a writers conference: it's a conference for writers. (All right, to be fair, I'll give one pair of examples showing that an apostrophe can make a difference. My friend Wells Hansen noticed that, if you're texting someone during the last part of a movie you've seen before, you would write *The best thing is it's ending*, if you're itching for it to be over, or *The best thing is its ending*, if the best bit is yet to come.)

Since the apostrophe is never going to be abolished, it should appear on children's letter blocks, and have its own Scrabble tile the way Q and X and Z do, and figure in crosswords as a letter. But it doesn't. Yet it's required in the spelling of a certain tiny set of words. And despite its uselessness, people are insanely preoccupied with seeing it used in the right places and not in the wrong ones. In 2001, an Englishman named John Richards set up an Apostrophe Protection Society dedicated to preserving it, as if it were some threatened species of tree frog. (At the end of 2019, he shut the society down, complaining that "laziness has won." The website immediately started getting six hundred times as much traffic as before. That's how completely nuts some people are about this objectively worthless pseudo-letter.)

I regret having to convey the thoroughly bad news that YOU REALLY HAVE TO LEARN TO PUT APOSTROPHES IN THE RIGHT PLACES. The only good news is that I can summarize what you have to know clearly and briefly.

1. Genitive NPs: The apostrophe is required in spelling the regular genitive suffix: the genitive singular -'s, as in _Gary's bike_ or the _president's_ signature, and the genitive plural -s', as in _the Yankees' victory_ or _all the cars' tail lights_.

Seven pronouns (*I*, *You*, *He*, *She*, *It*, *We*, *They*) are the only exceptions. They all have irregular genitive forms with no apostrophe (*my*, *your*, *his*, *her*, *its*, *our*, *their*). None of them use the regular -'s suffix. Remembering that will permit you to remember that the genitive pronoun *its* NEVER has an apostrophe: _The kitten was chasing its tail_, not ~~The kitten was chasing it's tail.~~ Getting that wrong is undoubtedly the most common apostrophe mistake of them all.

2. Reduced forms of auxiliaries: The apostrophe is used in the spelling of the reduced forms of auxiliary verbs in informal style. Most are reduced to a single consonant sound in speech. So when "it has" or "it is" gets reduced to _it's_, you must ALWAYS use an apostrophe.

The most important instances of reduced auxiliaries are: _I'd, I'll, I'm, I've, you'd, you'll, you're, you've, he'd, he'll, he's, she'd, she'll, she's, it'd, it'll, it's, we'd, we'll, we're, we've, they'd, they'll, they're, they've._

The form *'d* stands for either *had* or *would* and the form *'s* stands for either *is* or *has*. The rest are unambiguous: *'ll* stands for *will*, *'m* stands for *am*, *'re* stands for *are*, *'ve* stands for *have*.

3. The negative suffix *-n't*: The apostrophe is the middle letter of the suffix that forms negative auxiliary verbs: *-n't*. It most commonly appears in word-forms like *aren't*, *can't*, *couldn't*, *don't*, *hadn't*, *hasn't*, *haven't*, *isn't*, *mustn't*, *shouldn't*, *wasn't*, *weren't*, *won't*, and *wouldn't*. It also appears in the spelling of *ain't*, which is a (notoriously) non-standard form replacing *am not*, *aren't*, *isn't*, *haven't*, and *hasn't*.

4. Weird plurals: The stern warning on page 35 ("never use an apostrophe to form a plural") has a marginal exception. In a few instances, the result of simply adding an *s* looks too bizarre to bear, so an apostrophe is commonly used, as in *The a's and b's stand for positive integers*, or *His handwritten S's and 5's looked identical*, or *When she talked about the family it was all I's and me's instead of we's and us's*. In these rare cases, the apostrophe adds clarity – though some sticklers would object even to these uses.

5. Other miscellanea: Other uses of the apostrophe include its occurrence in a few family names like *D'Arcy* or *O'Connor*, and in phrases like *the '60s, one o'clock, rock 'n' roll*, and so on, and in written forms of colloquialisms like *c'mon* (for *come on*), *'s all right* (for *it's all right*), *d'ya think?* (for *do you think?*), and written representations of colloquialisms like *smokin'* and *bitchin'*.

Hyphens

Hyphens are rather like apostrophes in being always silent and annoyingly multi-purpose. Word processors distinguish two kinds: (i) the ones that are automatically inserted when right-margin justification needs to show that a word has been split across lines, and (ii) the ones you explicitly type in. We'll be concerned only with type (ii). They differ from apostrophes in that they have something of a grammatical role. The hyphen is a kind of separator.

What is most likely to make people worry about them is that they mark the boundary between the parts of some compound words but not others. A pair of words commonly used together, like *baby* and *sitter*, will first be written separately (*baby sitter*), then start being written with a hyphen (*baby-sitter*), and eventually perhaps be written with no space (*babysitter*). People who worry about being correct (or rather, about not being clearly incorrect) want to know which is the right spelling.

My advice would be to avoid being a fanatic about this. Unfortunately, even dictionaries are inconsistent on points of this sort. The best I can do is to tell you that the usual evolution involves a gradual progress in the direction of combining words with no space or hyphen. So if you think you may have seen all three of "web site" and "web-site" and "website," and you're really in doubt about which to use, I have a very simple piece of advice: opt for the third, because it'll be the newest.

Some idea of the triviality of the issue about whether to hyphenate can be gleaned from the fact that Google completely ignores the difference between (for example) the words *tree house*, *tree-house*, and *treehouse*, giving the same results for each (though for what it's worth, the spellings without the hyphen definitely seem to be more frequent now).

One important grammatical rule about hyphen use is that when two words make a modifier of a third, you normally need a hyphen between the first two, especially if the second word is a **participle**. Consider this example:

> *He decided to leave the equity-trading business but remain in equity research.*

There is a hyphen after the first occurrence of *equity* but not after the second. Why? Because in *equity-trading business* you have a two-word compound, *equity-trading*, formed of the noun *equity* and the participle *trading*, and the result modifies the noun *business* to make up the main part of an NP, *the equity-trading business*. In *equity research* you just have an NP in which *equity* on its own modifies *research*. There's no compound.

Don't obsess about this sort of thing either. Consult the usage in a source you trust, and follow that. Not everyone will agree with you, because there is significant variation: people often want there to be what J.R.R. Tolkien might have called One Rule to ring them all, but sometimes there isn't an easy rule covering every case. In general, the variation in hyphen use doesn't matter: the people who don't agree with you won't be consistent with each other. For example, *checkbook* seems to have completely replaced *check book*, while *gun shop* hardly ever appears as *gunshop*.

Even respectable print sources are not fully consistent, though. Checking a few million words of newspaper prose, I found eight instances of *wine glass* but also three of *wineglass*. (There was also one case of *wine-glass*, but that was in the phrase *the wine-glass demonstration*, so that follows the rule for connecting two words to make a modifier; the writer apparently had *wine glass* in mind.) That weighs heavily in favor of *wine glass*. But a study of *tea cup*, *tea-cup*, and *teacup* might come out differently. What I do know is that this is not a particularly important issue in how to write English. It's a matter of spelling, but not as important as the stuff about the letters from *a* to *z*.

Far more important than whether you decide you like *corn chip* or *corn-chip* or *cornchip* is whether you are consistent in your own use. Decide on one spelling you have seen in print and stick with it. Within one piece of writing you should only use one spelling for a specific word.

Novelists' spellings of casual speech

There are quite a few conventional spellings that novelists and other writers use to indicate casual pronunciations:

REDUCED FORM	FULL FORM
coulda or *could've*	*could have*
gimme	*give me*
gonna	*going to*
gotta	*got to*
hafta	*have to*
kinda	*kind of*
oughta	*ought to*
shoulda or *should've*	*should have*
sorta	*sort of*
wanna	*want to*
woulda or *would've*	*would have*

Punctuation

Punctuation is a system of conventions closely related to grammar, and not fully understandable without a grasp of grammar, but different from it in that syntax is natural, and applies to speech as well, but punctuation is governed by explicit conventions that publishers set down in style sheets and handbooks. Its function is to display structure in written material. It's not part of the content; it's there to guide you through the content and supply extra information about the parts of what you're reading. The punctuation marks used in contemporary written English are these:

period (= full stop)	.
question mark	?
exclamation mark	!
comma	,

semicolon	;
colon	:
dash	–
parentheses	(...)
square brackets	[...]
single quotation marks	' ... '
double quotation marks	" ... "

Neither the hyphen nor the apostrophe appears on this list, because they're part of the spelling system, not of the system for punctuating sentences.

Punctuation is purely a feature of written English, and has no simple or direct relation to either grammar or speech. It's a separate system of sometimes rather strict rules for marking structure in sentences. Commas and periods do tend to correspond to slight pauses or phrasing boundaries in speech, but not very reliably; question marks do tend to occur on the ends of independent interrogative clauses, and perhaps indicate rising pitch in speech, but not invariably; exclamation marks don't necessarily signify either exclamative clause type or excited shouting; and quotation marks, which have other uses besides enclosing quotations, don't have any normal correlate in speech at all.

The rules of punctuation are firmly fixed and must be learned in full. You have hardly any latitude to vary things at will. Most of syntax varies a bit from style to style, or even speaker to speaker, which gives you room for negotiation on what should be called correct or standard; but punctuation is far more codified. It's a matter of fairly clear and sharp conventions. If you don't follow the usual rules, people will make negative judgments about you from your writing. So I may sound a bit more dogmatic in this chapter than elsewhere; the judgy sort of people who are waiting out there to size you up and put you down are going to jump all over you if you make punctuation errors.

What's more, it can be extremely important in real-life terms. Millions of dollars have been won or lost in legal cases because of a single punctuation mark in a contract or a statute.

Fortunately, the punctuation system can be readily studied from the evidence in printed works. The foremost of these is, by popular acclaim, *The Chicago Manual of Style*, published by the University of Chicago Press (17th edition out by 2017 and an 18th on the way). It covers punctuation in chapter 6 and spelling in chapter 7. All I'm going to do here is underline a few points that are insufficiently recognized.

Sentence-enders: periods, question marks, and exclamation marks

The **period** (or **full stop**) is, as everyone knows, the standard way to mark the end of a sentence with a main clause that is not interrogative:

This discussion has gone on too long.

This is obligatory in every kind of writing except at the end of (i) a newspaper headline or (ii) the last sentence of an informal email or text message.

The **question mark** is used to mark the end of a clause that expresses a direct question:

Is there any real point to this discussion?   [closed interrogative]
What is the real point of this discussion?   [open interrogative]

It might sometimes be employed at the end of a subordinate interrogative clause, but usually not. This sentence shouldn't have a question mark, because it makes a statement about an attitude to a question rather than asking the question:

I have been wondering whether there is any real point to this discussion.

There is a small amount of flexibility, even with independent interrogatives. A sentence in which the main clause is interrogative can sometimes end with a period, especially if it doesn't invite an answer at all, or is intended to signal what the writer thinks is the obvious answer:

Isn't that just the stupidest idea you ever heard.

The **exclamation mark** is used as a substitute for the period at the end of a declarative main clause, conveying that it is supposed to be surprising, exciting, noteworthy, or highly emphatic:

That is absolutely the stupidest idea I ever heard!

In serious writing, this is rare. If you use exclamation marks too much, you may seem to be writing like an airhead. It certainly isn't true that either imperative or exclamative main clauses have to end with an exclamation mark. These sentences are far better left without one:

Come to my office later to get the details.   [imperative]
What an absolutely ridiculous idea it was.   [exclamative]

Particularly when writing nonfiction on serious topics (essays for a history professor, reports to shareholders, etc.), exclamation marks are to be avoided. Teachers hate them, and shareholders aren't likely to think much of them either.

Commas

The comma is a sentence-internal minor boundary marker, not a sentence-ender. It optionally marks the end of a clause-initial adjunct:

> *With the possible exception of New York, London is the world's*
> *most important financial center.*

The comma in that case is very helpful, because it prevents the words *New York London* from coming together in a confusing clump. The same is true in this pair of examples, where the first has a confusing sequence of identical phrases and the second reads much more easily:

> *?If you really think you can do it do it.*
> *If you really think you can do it, do it.*

A comma obligatorily marks both ends of a parenthetical interruption such as a supplementary relative clause. Parentheses or dashes can be used instead, but commas are the most common device. This example has two parenthetical interruptions, both underlined:

> *The rest of us, <u>still a bit annoyed</u>, were now, <u>at last</u>, beginning to forgive him.*

The basic fact expressed is that the rest of us were beginning to forgive him, but the sentence is interrupted twice, first by a supplement consisting of an AdjP (*still a bit annoyed*), and second by a PP functioning as adjunct (*at last*), telling us that it had taken rather a long time to arrive at forgiveness. Both of those are presented as asides, not the main content.

Some people seem to think you should never have a comma before a coordinator unless what follows is an independent clause. That assumption is apparently built into Microsoft Word's grammar checker. It isn't true: there is no rigid rule. This is from the script of Oscar Wilde's play *The Importance of Being Earnest*:

> *And now I'll have a cup of tea, and one of those nice cucumber sandwiches you promised me.*

Oscar knew when to write a comma. On the other hand, you definitely wouldn't want a comma after *tea* in this sentence:

Tea and cucumber sandwiches will be served at 4 p.m.

Most of the time, there's plenty of optionality about the use of commas. Or to put that another way, most of the time there's plenty of optionality about the use of commas. But length and complexity can sometimes influence things. In this pair of examples, the first doesn't need a comma before *I decided*, whereas the second really does:

The following day I decided to confront him.
After spending three whole days on the island without any explanation of what my role was supposed to be, I decided to confront him.

No comma between subject and verb

One place you should NOT put a comma is between the subject and the VP in a declarative clause. Things were different in the 18th century, but for well over a hundred years now it has been a rule of punctuation that even a long subject does not have a comma separating it from the VP. This sentence has quite a long subject (eleven words):

The only metal always in liquid state at normal room temperature is mercury.

Even so, it's still not acceptable under contemporary standards to follow it with a comma:

~~The only metal always in liquid state at normal room temperature, is mercury.~~

Rare exceptions for specific reasons may be found. When I first read this in *The Economist*, I simply couldn't understand it:

*That what should have been fairly accessible, given both the price
and the number of Popeyes locations across the country, was not
only heightened its appeal.*

I had to go back and work for several seconds on figuring
out how it could possibly be grammatical. The words *not
only* fit so naturally together, which encouraged me to try to
interpret *not only heightened its appeal* as a phrase, but then
nothing made sense. After long moments of bafflement, and
a careful re-reading of the context, I finally saw how I was
supposed to understand it. The subject is this content clause:

that what should have been fairly accessible was not

The phrase *was not* is meant to be understood as *was not
accessible*. It's followed by a long parenthetical phrase: *given
both the price and the number of Popeyes locations across the
country*. Finally we reach the VP:

only heightened its appeal

So the sentence is saying that something should have been accessible but wasn't, and this lack of accessibility merely increased its
appeal to the public. The sentence was definitely not well written.
Adding a comma at the end of the long subject NP (normally a
grammatical error) would have improved it immensely:

*That what should have been fairly accessible, given both the price
and the number of Popeyes locations across the country, was not,
only heightened its appeal.*

But that's a highly unusual and exceptional case. The result
with the added comma still isn't great. The whole sentence
should have been rethought and rewritten.

Another case where you just might want to add an exceptional comma after a subject NP would be to break up an
otherwise strange-looking repetition like *play it play it*:

[?]Let's have someone who really knows how to play it play it.

Or you might want to redesign the sentence completely. You decide; you're the designer. But only decide after you've put yourself in the shoes of the reader, perhaps by reading aloud what you've written.

The run-on sentence or comma splice

A very common mistake in writing is the type of sentence known as a comma splice or run-on sentence. It involves two independent clauses linked by a comma, which is hardly ever grammatical:

> ~~Several people suggested that the resolution should be withdrawn, yesterday the Executive Committee decided to do that.~~

Don't do this. It's ungrammatical because a comma has been used to link two independent clauses (that is, clauses that could stand in their own right as sentences). One way to correct this would be to replace the comma with a period and start a new sentence after it:

> *Several people suggested that the resolution should be withdrawn. Yesterday the Executive Committee decided to do that.*

The other way to fix it would be to use a **semicolon** instead of the comma, so let's deal with that next.

Semicolons

The key difference between a semicolon (;) and a comma (,) is that a semicolon can separate two independent clauses in a sentence, like this:

> *Several people suggested that the resolution should be withdrawn; yesterday the Executive Committee decided to do that.*

It is used most often when there is a strong topic link between the two clauses. Take this example, from near the beginning of H.G. Wells's novel *The War of the Worlds*:

> *I never dreamed of it then as I watched; no one on earth dreamed of that unerring missile.*

These could have been presented as separate sentences, with a period at the end of the first, but the semicolon brings them closer together, drawing attention to the similarity of their content – they both have **Dream** as the main verb, and are both about the way humans had never dreamed that Martians might be headed toward Earth.

A different but important use of the semicolon is as a kind of promoted comma. A comma-separated list of items with commas in them can look very confusing, but that can be fixed by promoting the main separators from comma to semicolon:

> *Alma Maria Schindler was successively married to Gustav Mahler, the great Austro-Bohemian romantic composer; Walter Gropius, the German architect, founder of the Bauhaus school; and Franz Werfel, the Austro-Bohemian novelist, playwright, and poet.*

Without the semicolons that mark off the accomplishments of the successive spouses, the sentence would be a bewildering welter of phrases and commas. The semicolons break it up nicely into statements about each of Alma's three husbands, which allows comma-separated parenthetical descriptions within those statements.

Colons

The colon is most commonly used to separate an independent clause from something it sets us up to expect, especially if it's some kind of list, or a piece of quoted speech.

The Benelux Union comprises three countries: Belgium, the Netherlands, and Luxembourg.
As I drew nearer I heard Stent's voice: "Keep back! Keep back!"

A very specific rule enforced (for example) by the editors of *The New York Times* is that if an **independent clause** follows a colon, it should begin with a capital letter:

Remember one strict rule about rice: You should never re-heat cooked rice that has been left for several hours at room temperature.

Clearly, this rule requires the user to know the difference between an independent clause (one that could stand alone as a sentence) and other kinds of constituent. Some publishers adopt this rule from *The Times*, but some don't. British ones generally do not. I haven't followed it in this book: they can't make me.

Dashes

The dash is primarily used as a way of marking off a supplement that is more dramatic than a mere comma, especially one that's more radically disruptive of the sentence, such as a full independent clause. In the following example, the supplement between the dashes is not just a constituent of the whole sentence with pauses around it, but a completely different sentence that breaks in from nowhere and could almost be an intervention by another voice:

The Martians seem to have calculated their descent with amazing subtlety – their mathematical learning is evidently far in excess of ours – and to have carried out their preparations with a well-nigh perfect unanimity.

This would actually be ungrammatical if we replaced the dashes by commas.

Some printed works use an en dash ("–"), with spaces on each side. Others use the slightly longer em dash ("—"), usually without spaces. So you might find either of these, depending on the publisher:

Few of them are religious – not that it matters.
Few of them are religious—not that it matters.

Parentheses

The round parenthesis markers "(" and ")" are of course used to mark off side remarks and interruptions of the main flow embedded within sentences or paragraphs:

Miss Swift (who, incidentally, is not related to Taylor Swift) was not very pleased to learn what had happened.

But where the final punctuation for a sentence goes can be important. If I may paraphrase an advertising slogan about things people do in Las Vegas, WHAT STARTS INSIDE PAREN-THESES STAYS INSIDE PARENTHESES. If you start a sentence with a capital letter after a left parenthesis, you've got to finish it before the right parenthesis, and if you start a sentence outside a pair of parentheses, the punctuation mark that ends it must be outside those parentheses. Notice the periods at the ends of these two examples:

Miss Swift was not very pleased to learn what had happened (and incidentally, she is not related to Taylor Swift).

Miss Swift was not very pleased to learn what had happened. (Incidentally, she is not related to Taylor Swift.)

Square brackets

In rare cases you might need to have a parenthesis inside a larger parenthesis, and in such cases the inner one can be put in square brackets. But the main use of square brackets is to enclose interpolated comments when you as the writer have to clarify something inside a quotation. A common case of this sort involves inserting the Latin word "sic" (meaning "thus") inside a direct quotation to signal that the preceding word is peculiar or perhaps mistaken, but that's how it appeared in the original:

> *Seemingly heedless of the role of women in the modern army, the general announced: "I am sure that every soldier will do his [sic] duty."*

Quotation marks

Whether to use single or double quotation marks to mark off directly quoted speech or writing is usually up to the publisher or editor; and whichever they prefer, the other can be used for quotations inside quotations. Quotation marks are also used to mark words that are mentioned rather than used in a sentence. This example illustrates single-quoted words inside a quotation marked with double quotation marks:

> *Mary McCarthy was sued for saying about Lillian Hellman: "Every word she writes is a lie, including 'and' and 'the'."*

I put the period that ends Mary McCarthy's remark inside the double quotation marks, but outside the single quotation marks round *the*. But the position of periods and commas relative to quotation marks is a notorious point of divergence between American and British publishing preferences.

American publishers virtually always demand that a period or comma after a quotation must be pushed inside the quotation even if logically it doesn't belong there. British publishers also often prefer single quotation marks. So you might find that a British book or newspaper has *I called him 'sir'*, obviously, while an American publisher might prefer *I called him "sir,"* *obviously.*

I like the logic of the British style here, because as a linguist I have to mention words and phrases inside quotation marks so often. But don't try arguing about this with a publisher's editor, because it won't go well. Publishers are stubborn on this point. In fact they will get mean and ugly.

Capitalization

There is a sense in which making the first letter of a word a capital (upper-case) letter is a kind of surrogate for punctuation: it's obligatory in English to capitalize the first letter of a sentence, so a capital letter can indicate the beginning of a sentence (including a quoted sentence) in the same way that a period can indicate its end – though of course proper nouns also need a capital initial, so a capital letter only signals a new sentence when there isn't an alternative reason for its being capitalized.

Two clauses with the very same words may differ in which one gets an initial capital, because a clause can be just part of a sentence. Notice the difference between the grammatical sentences and the ungrammatical ones in this set:

> *Night is falling; it will soon be dark.*
> ~~*Night is falling. it will soon be dark.*~~
> ~~*Night is falling; It will soon be dark.*~~
> *"Night is falling," said Wilson; "It will soon be dark."*

18

Style

Style is a much more subtle matter than grammar, and this is a book about grammar, so I will have very little to say here; just enough to underline the differences.

In grammar, there's often just one answer to a question: *The party's over* is grammatical and ~~Party's the over~~ is not, and that's that. No room for argument. But when we consider style, you'll nearly always face a range of choices about the way to put things. Get the style wrong, and your writing may seem ugly or silly or clunky or inept, but it won't strictly be erroneous.

Ultimately you'll want to write in your own style. Advice about the style others might have chosen will be of little use to you once you're a skilled writer. But there is a great deal of educative value in looking at examples of various styles and comparing them.

A steak can be unpalatable either because it's cold and raw or because it's burned to a crisp, and in the same way your style in a particular piece of writing could be wrong in multiple ways for its intended purpose or audience or topic. For example, you can be so casual you sound sloppy, or so formal that you sound pompous. Both extremes are usually bad from any perspective. But there's a broad middle zone where the style suits the content well enough that most people won't even notice it. And that's often what you want: a writing style shouldn't necessarily call attention to itself. Here are five examples of steadily increasing formality:

Where you're from ain't gonna make no nevermind.	Far too informal except when writing dialog; *ain't* is stereotypically non-standard.
Couldn't care less where you're from.	Thoroughly casual; notice the dropped main clause subject.
It doesn't matter a bit where you come from.	Moderately normal style; not definitively either formal or casual.
It does not matter at all where you come from.	Clearly formal; notice "does not" – yet the stranded preposition is still required.
It is of scant importance what your geographic origin may be.	Too formal for many purposes; sounds pompous.

The middle of the range is the acceptable part; the far ends are the inedible extremes. The way to get used to style differences of this sort is to read a lot, and pay attention to how things are phrased in different kinds of text. Read people's text messages, and personal emails, and business letters, and detective novels, and serious nonfiction, and compare them.

Here are two sample paragraphs, fairly extreme in each of the two directions: a paragraph that's definitely formal (maybe too much so) followed by a paragraph saying much the same thing but in much closer to a normal way of writing (perhaps a bit too casual).

RATHER TOO FORMAL

This paragraph is intentionally cast in an unusually formal style, the tone of which might be judged inappropriate for correspondence intended for anyone with whom one is personally acquainted. Highly formal style can be somewhat alienating for the reader, conveying a sense of social distance or even pomposity rather than of directness and clarity. It would thus constitute a grievous error to equate formal style with grammatical correctness, as is sometimes done by misguided teachers and less perceptive style and usage guides. Instruction of that kind would risk inculcating in schoolchildren a perception of their educational institution as culturally alien. The range of distinct style options in Standard English constitutes a resource in the use of which a skilled writer should be well versed. To imagine that only the most formal style is correct would be to misvalue and squander that resource.

A BIT TOO CASUAL

I've written this bit in totally informal style. Too informal, you might say. But informality isn't the same as error. Just because some feature (like using "I'm" or "isn't") is informal style doesn't mean it's not good Standard English. Lots of wasted time and effort in English teaching goes into trying to get schoolkids to write more formally by telling them that everyday words or phrases are "wrong" or "not proper English." Overstatements like that just make kids think school is dumb. Teaching formal ways of writing that don't occur so much in ordinary talk is all very well, but that doesn't make it right to tell lies about English, like that there's no such word as "can't," or that "Who else did you talk to?" is a grammar mistake. The range of different style choices available in English gives you a nice box of writer's tools. If you think only formal style is "correct," you're throwing half of that toolbox away. If you want your writing to feel natural, there's more than one Standard English style to be aware of.

Although style is a matter of appropriateness to context, there are a few general properties that almost guarantee people won't like a piece of writing. One of them is verbosity – pointless wordiness. People tend to react negatively to that. If you can see how something could have been said using distinctly fewer words, it's almost always a good idea to consider rewriting. Nobody likes padding or blathering, and almost all how-to-write books warn against it. Here are four triples of examples, each with a long version, a medium one, and a shorter one, but all three versions saying essentially the same thing:

WORDY: *One should ideally aim at achieving a close approach to employing minimal quantities of unnecessary verbiage.*
MEDIUM: *Attempt to get rid of words that are not really needed.*
TERSE: *Omit needless words.*

WORDY: *On and on the little yappy dog kept barking, yap yap yap yap yap.*
MEDIUM: *The little dog carried on yapping.*
TERSE: *The dog yapped on.*

WORDY: *In the background behind him, a large array of all sorts of different scientific instruments was clearly visible.*
MEDIUM: *Behind him was a large assortment of scientific equipment.*
TERSE: *Behind him was some equipment.*

WORDY: *Cerium is a chemical element that has the symbol Ce and has the atomic number 58. It is a soft, ductile, silvery-white metallic element that tarnishes slowly when it is exposed to air. It is so soft that you can actually cut it with an ordinary knife.*
MEDIUM: *Cerium is a soft, ductile, silvery-white metallic element with symbol Ce and atomic number 58. It tarnishes when exposed to air and is soft enough that it can be cut with a knife.*
TERSE: *Cerium (Ce, atomic number 58), a soft, ductile, silvery metal that tarnishes in air, is soft enough to cut with a knife.*

Whether to pick a longer or shorter version will depend on the context and purpose, but very often a medium or terse version will be preferable. The point is that you should never risk wasting your reader's time or straining their attention. This is a particular danger when (as with college homework essays or term papers) you have been assigned a minimum length limit. Never forget, if you get your paper over the minimum by padding with unnecessary words and phrases, the instructor who reads it will probably notice, and will hate you for it. To make a piece of writing longer, think up more genuine content. Pushing in extra words and phrases to bloat up what little you've got won't earn you any praise!

Other published writing, especially literature, should be used as a guide to style only with great care. Charles Dickens famously wrote bloated, humorously verbose sentences (he was, after all, being paid by the word for the serializations of his stories), and people loved him. But average sentence length in English has been falling for several hundred years now, and readers will not be grateful for hugely long sentences. Lee Child, for example, writes a lot of the time in very short sentences ("Reacher said nothing"), and his Jack Reacher novels have sold over 100 million copies so far. (I've heard a Jack Reacher novel sells somewhere in the world roughly every ten seconds.)

Any writer should read widely in the relevant kinds of work (novels, newspaper columns, business memos, academic papers, whatever is the relevant genre), and make conscious decisions about the feel each sentence should have. Sometimes, perhaps, you might want to write luxuriantly long sentences, but other times it might be a lot better to write like Lee Child. Or mix the sentence styles up. But it's your choice; don't let anyone bully you into doing it their way.

Dangling modifiers

The so-called "dangling modifier" or "dangling participle" is a writing flaw so subtle that it can't really be called a grammar error; it's more like a failure of empathy. But it's so interesting it wouldn't be fair not to discuss it here. To get the feel of it, read this example:

> *?Being six feet tall, there was nothing that could be done.*

There's a strangeness about it, a feeling of puzzlement due to incompleteness. You're left thinking, "WHO was six feet tall?"

Here's what's going on. When a main clause begins with a subjectless predicative adjunct like *being six feet tall,* the reader (or hearer, for that matter) needs to figure out who it's talking about. If the property of being six feet tall is being mentioned, we're going to need to know who is claimed to have that property. But in the example above, nobody else is mentioned, so we're baffled. The subjectless clause *being six feet tall* just hangs there, dangling, unable to contribute to a coherent meaning. But now compare it with this:

> *Being six feet tall, Justin could easily reach the box.*

Now the same initial clause is perfect: the subject of the main clause is *Justin*, and there's nothing to conflict with the idea that Justin is the six-footer, so, quick as a flash, we adopt that assumption, and things are fine.

Now one more contrast. Take a look at this sentence:

> *Being six feet tall, the box was easy for Justin to reach.*

Now it's weird again, though perhaps not as weird as the first example. The strategy we used above – look for the subject of the main clause and see if that makes sense as the subject – lets us down. For a split second, you think you're being told about a six-foot-tall box. You rapidly decide that can't be right, and move on to find a more suitable entity that's six feet tall. It must be Justin. But you still have a subconscious feeling of being momentarily baffled: you were doing your best to understand the sentence and you were sent down a blind alley. The problem is not that *being six feet tall* is dangling with no subject; rather, it's the exact opposite: instead of dangling uninterpretably, it gets connected up to the wrong NP, and you have to undo that connection and give the situation a rethink.

If you keep your eyes open when reading, and keep your ears open when listening to other people's speech (especially prepared speech), you will find that it is enormously common for people to construct sentences like the third example above. Here's one from a news report about Brandon Calloway, an electrical engineering graduate who got badly beaten by the police after a traffic stop:

> *On July 16, while driving to his father's home, police in Oakland, Tennessee, beat Calloway after stopping him for a minor traffic violation and pursuit.*

Here, *while driving to his father's home* is an adjunct in which the *driving* clause has no subject. The subject of the main clause is *police in Oakland, Tennessee.* But it wasn't the police who were driving to Calloway's father's home! You're likely to have a moment of puzzlement when you read this, searching backward and forward for a suitable NP before finally settling on *Calloway.*

Sometimes you will come upon cases where the untensed subjectless adjunct clause is readily understandable as having the speaker or writer as its subject. For example, one author wrote:

> *Reading as an outsider, these parents seem to have collectively lost their minds.*

But in the context it is easy enough to see that this means "As I read things, these parents seem to me to have collectively lost their minds." You can readily forgive the author for not being explicit about that.

Other cases don't seem so excusable. The *Daily Mirror,* a British newspaper, said this about a young woman called Angel Lynn, who was kidnapped by her thuggish boyfriend Chay Bowskill:

> *The 20-year-old was filmed carrying Angel across a busy street and throwing her into the back of a van, but on speeding off at 60mph she fell from the vehicle.*

When you first read the words *on speeding off at 60mph she fell from the vehicle*, it seems for a moment as if *she* might be the intended subject of the subjectless adjunct clause *speeding off at 60mph*. But it wasn't Angel who sped off, it was Bowskill. All poor Angel did was fall out of the van Bowskill was carrying her off in.

Such instances of bad writing are amazingly common. They're almost too common to be regarded as accidental grammatical mistakes. They look to me like failures of courtesy: cases in which the writer failed to consider whether the reader might misunderstand. So, if you can muster the necessary discipline, always ask yourself that question. Read your work over, and reconsider the comprehensibility of every sentence you've written.

Further reading

I cannot offer even the beginnings of an introduction to all the thousands of other books, and tens of thousands of journal articles, that have been written about English grammar, usage, and style. Even just trying to acknowledge the ones that have influenced my thinking would consume way too much space. So what you see below is just a few brief hints at where you might go next if the subject intrigues you, plus a few sharp opinions about books I think you should avoid. I won't follow full scholarly bibliography practice here (where you carefully point out things like that Cambridge University Press is located in Cambridge – duh!), but I'll give enough details that with modern web tools you'll have no difficulty tracking down the books I mention.

Grammar

The first port of call for anyone who wants to delve more seriously into this book's modern approach to English grammar would be *A Student's Introduction to English Grammar* by Rodney Huddleston, Geoffrey K. Pullum, and Brett Reynolds

(2nd edition, Cambridge University Press, 2022). It's a 400-page undergraduate-level textbook that's fully compatible with this book in its theoretical assumptions, but it goes into a lot more detail. It's not elementary, but then if you have read this book you are not exactly a beginner anymore.

That textbook is based on a much larger and more advanced work: *The Cambridge Grammar of the English Language* (by Rodney Huddleston and Geoffrey K. Pullum et al., Cambridge University Press, 2002) – the book I've been referring to as *CGEL*. It's a large scholarly reference work (over 1,800 pages), and although it doesn't presuppose a linguistics degree, it uses more technical concepts and vocabulary than this book, and it attempts to be complete and exhaustive. It's intended for grammarians and designers of courses rather than for students or for the casual reader. It's designed for looking things up, so in addition to an index of topics, there's a lexical index to help you find the specific pages on which the grammatical properties of certain words are discussed.

Among the literally thousands of other books on English grammar published over the last four hundred years, most are the sort of books I've been warning you about. Hordes of them, merrily plagiarizing each other, repeating tired myths, vague waffle, and useless definitions. A few are worth getting to know, but many are not. Sadly, the very best are now more than a hundred years old, which is a problem: even though language change is slow, a century is long enough for the language to have altered a bit even in syntax. Anyone with historical interests will want to read widely in the earlier grammatical literature, to see exactly what it says in classic books by such scholars as Ann Fisher (*A Practical New Grammar*, 1750), Robert Lowth (*A Short Introduction to English Grammar*, 1762), Lindley Murray (*English Grammar Adapted to the Different Classes of Learners*, 1795), Goold Brown (*The Grammar of English Grammars*, 1851), Henry Sweet (*A New English Grammar*, 2 volumes, 1892–1898), or Otto Jespersen

(*A Modern English Grammar*, 7 volumes, 1909–1949). But don't expect their terminology and assumptions to agree with this book. Huddleston and I spent many long years thinking carefully about why and how we were going to say goodbye to many assumptions and terms in the pre-2000 literature.

Usage

One of the finest desk reference books for controversial points of usage and correctness in English is *Merriam-Webster's Dictionary of English Usage* (often called *MWDEU*), ed. by E. Ward Gilman et al. (Merriam-Webster, Springfield, Conn., 1989). A newer and more compactly presented edition of it appeared in 2002 as *Merriam-Webster's Concise Dictionary of English Usage*. It's strikingly non-judgmental, hardly ever telling you how you ought to write. It certainly never tells you that you're a bad person if you disobey the rules. Its aim is to tell you what really goes on out there in the world of English literature and journalism, giving copious history and examples. My treatment of usage issues in chapter 16 of this book is no more than a brief sampling, but whenever you want detail on the background of some controversial point of grammar that I don't cover, turn to *MWDEU*, which covers a thousand times as much. As you get used to it, you'll find you can guess where to turn in its alphabetically ordered entries (for stranding, you look up "Preposition at end," etc.). On the few occasions where I mentioned specific 18th- or 19th-century grammarians earlier in this book, you will soon be able to track down the relevant works using the bibliography at the end of *MWDEU*.

The most complete guide to American English usage is *Garner's Modern English Usage* (by Bryan A. Garner, 5th edition, Oxford University Press, New York, 2022). It is a superb reference book, extraordinarily wide-ranging and extremely detailed. It's much more conservative and directive than *MWDEU*, supplying firm advice against many commonly encountered words, phrases, or constructions. But the recommendations are generally quite sensible, because (and how rare this is!) they are backed up not just by personal opinions or peeves but by detailed surveys of the evidence. If Garner advises that you shouldn't use some word or grammatical pattern, he will have checked his advice with evidence from online searches or surveys. On grammar, he follows the 19th-century tradition, not the more modern analyses and terminology that I have introduced in this book, so you will see him using terminology that I have explicitly rejected; but that's true for almost every book on the market, and it doesn't stop Garner's from being an indispensable reference book for any serious writer.

People will tell you that the ultimate guide is H.W. Fowler's *A Dictionary of Modern English Usage*, but it would be most unwise to believe them. Fowler was an interesting scholar, but he formed his ideas around the time of the First World War, and the 1st edition of his book was in 1926. That's just too long ago – nearly a century. Trust *MWDEU* and Garner.

Style

Perhaps the most linguistically intelligent modern study of writing style and its linguistic and psychological roots is *The Sense of Style: The Thinking Person's Guide to Writing in the 21st Century*, by Steven Pinker (Allen Lane, London, 2014). Pinker is a fine writer on language himself, and his grammar assumptions are mostly compatible with this book (hence with *CGEL*). He gives some well-explained scientific details about why certain kinds of sentence are better style than others. On page 205 you can see what I would call an error – a glaring case of an item being assigned to the wrong category (finding it is left as a fun exercise for the reader of this book!), but, hey, humans make mistakes. The book in general is beautiful, and everyone interested in how English works should read it.

Joseph Williams's book *Style: Toward Clarity and Grace* is also well worth reading. It has gone through numerous editions since he first conceived it, and you will find a dozen different editions on sale, with different dates, co-authors, and publishers. Some have slightly modified titles. I won't pick from this dizzying array; I'll just say that Williams is sensible about language and worth reading.

Another excellent book on style, of a very different kind, is *The Sound on the Page: Great Writers Talk About Style and Voice in Writing*, by Ben Yagoda (HarperCollins, New York, 2005). It features interviews with more than forty diverse authors discussing their own style of writing.

The books above are about style in the literary sense: how you deploy the resources of grammar to get a point across. For style in the very different nitty-gritty sense involving punctuation, font choice, citation, and other aspects of manuscript preparation, the place to turn is *The Chicago Manual of Style* (University of Chicago Press). The 17th edition appeared in 2017, and an 18th is in preparation. It is matchlessly authoritative and rightly revered.

Disrecommendations

Now for a few remarks that are just between you, me, and the gatepost. It may upset millions, but I owe it to you to speak the truth. Some of the most famous and much-loved books on how to write are grossly misinformed on grammar and usage, not to be trusted on style, and way past their use-by dates, which are spread across the 20th century.

A flagrant case is the book commonly known as *The Elements of Style*. It's actually E.B. White's revision and expansion of a 1918 book by William Strunk called *Elements of Style*, which

White was assigned when he was in one of Strunk's classes at Cornell in 1919. Parts of it were four decades old when White published his version with Macmillan in 1959, and they are over a century old now, after several more editions by different publishers. Much of what it says about grammar and usage is very bad advice, and some of White's changes and additions (which Strunk never saw) are flagrant nonsense – like when White says that stranding a preposition "sounds like murder" (4th edition, page 78). Stay away from this book.

George Orwell's "Politics and the English language" (1946) is an essay, not a book, but millions of students will have seen it in a book because it was reprinted at least 118 times in 325 editions of fifty-eight college readers between 1952 and 1996 (see "The essay canon" by Lynn Bloom in *College English* 61.4, 1999, 401–430). Its text can be found in scores of places on the web, and hordes of English teachers have been singing its praises for three-quarters of a century. It is full of sanctimonious virtue signaling, dishonestly cherry-picked examples, and dumb advice about writing that no one follows, like that you should never use any familiar phrase, and of course that you should never use the passive (when his own essay uses the passive far more than most writing in English does). My advice: don't even read it, but if an English teacher asks, pretend you think it's wonderful.

William Zinsser's *On Writing Well* is a much-praised book on writing, first published in 1976 and reissued in a 30th-Anniversary Edition by HarperCollins in 2006. It tells you that most adjectives are "unnecessary" and most adverbs are too, which is flagrantly untrue (see chapters 8 and 9 of this book), and its objection to beginning a sentence with *However* is that "it hangs there like a wet dishrag" (page 73). If you think this sounds like sensible advice, that makes exactly one of us. I'm not a fan.

I'm also not a fan of *On Writing: A Memoir of the Craft* by the great horror-story writer Stephen King (a 20th-Anniversary

Edition was published by Scribner in 2020), though some people think it's a wonderful book. On grammar and usage he is just silly. He thinks adverbs are like dandelions and will spread uncontrollably if you don't stamp them out (page 125) – but then (as I said in chapter 9) he goes ahead and uses them just like everybody else does, probably without realizing it.

All these works are clueless about grammar, dogmatic in tone, and absurdly out of date. Shun them. But don't ever tell anyone I said that, because all of these authors have millions of devoted admirers who will mark me out as an enemy, and I don't want that.

Glossary

accusative the form for a non-**subject** pronoun, e.g. *me* or *them*.

active not of the **passive** type; clauses like *Various errors occurred* and *I shot the sheriff* are active clauses.

adjective word of the category exemplified by *enthusiastic, proud, reprehensible, recent, big,* etc.

adverb word of the category exemplified by *enthusiastically, proudly, reprehensibly, recently, soon,* etc.

article one of the two most basic determinatives, *the* and *a(n)*.

attributive functioning as a modifier before a noun in an NP, as in *good dog*.

auxiliary verb **verb** belonging to the subcategory that can precede the subject in an interrogative main clause.

category class of words with common grammatical characteristics, e.g. **noun**, **verb**, **adjective**, etc.

clause minimal constituent capable of expressing a statement or question; in English, virtually always contains a **verb**.

closed interrogative interrogative clause allowing only a closed set of potentially appropriate answers, like *Do you come here often?*, where the list of appropriate answers is assumed to contain just *Yes* and *No*.

comparative   the version of an **adjective** or **adverb** that is used to express being further along some scale: *higher, louder, faster, more.*

conjunction   see **coordinator.**

connective adjunct   an **adjunct** like the **adverb** *consequently* or the **PP** *of course*, often used to connect a sentence to the previous one in a discourse.

coordinator   word such as *and* or *but*, used for linking two phrases or clauses together with equal status. [Many linguists call them "conjunctions," but that's not a good choice of term, because the coordinator *or* expresses logical disjunction, not conjunction.]

count noun   common noun denoting a countable kind of thing and hence typically having a plural form, e.g. *Dog* (*two dogs*), *City* (*several cities*), *Mistake* (*repeated mistakes*).

declarative   clause of the type that is most typically used to express a statement (*They were very kind*).

definite   (of an NP) referring to something specific and in principle identifiable, as with *that arrangement* or *my arrangement*, rather than non-specific like *an arrangement.*

determinative   member of the class of words exemplified by *an, all, each, most, several, some, the.* [Many linguists call them "determiners," but we need one term for the category of determinatives and a different one for the function **determiner** (of).]

determiner   the function of the constituent required before singular count nouns (and permitted with other common nouns) in NPs, like the underlined parts of *the spider's web* or *our secret* or *hardly any point*. Not to be confused with the category **determinative.**

direct object   an **object** typically denoting an affected entity or something transferred, like the underlined NP in *hand the usher your ticket.*

exclamative   clause of the type that is most typically used to express an exclamatory statement (*How kind they were!*).

feminine   belonging to the gender class that agrees with the pronoun *She* rather than *He* or *It*.

gender   the property that distinguishes classes like **masculine** vs. **feminine** vs. **neuter** (*He* / *She* / *It*) or **human** vs. **non-human** (*Who* / *Which*).

genitive   the form of an NP that is marked by *-'s* (or *-s'* for regular genitive plurals), like *John's*, or the irregular counterpart for a pronoun (e.g. *his*). [Many linguists use the term "possessive" instead of "genitive," but that's not a good choice of term, because in many cases its meaning has nothing to do with possession.]

gerund-participle   the form of a **verb** that ends in *-ing*, as in *singing*.

head   principal member of a phrase, often obligatory, which determines the grammatical properties of the whole phrase; e.g. the **verb** in a **VP** or the **preposition** in a **PP**.

human   the usual term for the gender class including words for referring to members of the genus *Homo* and other person-like entities (androids, robots).

imperative   clause of the type that is most typically used to express a directive such as an order or a suggestion (*Be kind.*).

indefinite   the property an NP has when what it refers to is open and unspecified rather than specific and in principle identifiable, as with *some arrangement, a former pope, most shirts*.

indirect object   an **object** typically denoting a recipient or beneficiary, like the underlined NP in *hand <u>the usher</u> your ticket*.

inflection   modified form dependent on some grammatically relevant aspect of the context.

interjection   word belonging to the small category of words mostly used as indicators of speaker emotion rather than part of the structure of a sentence: *Ah, Hey, Ooh, Ouch, Ugh, Wow*.

interrogative clause of the type that is most typically used to pose a question (*Were they kind?* or *How kind were they?*).

irregular not belonging to a class that follows a general rule-governed pattern, especially in inflection.

lexeme word in the sense that is relevant for adding entries to the dictionary: an entry is provided for the lexeme *Take*, but not for its separate word-forms *take, taken, takes, taking,* and *took.*

lexical verb non-**auxiliary verb**.

masculine belonging to the gender class that agrees with the pronoun *He* rather than *She* or *It.*

mass noun noun that denotes a kind of concrete, abstract, or metaphorical stuff (*Zinc, Water, Innocence*), not a type of countable thing (*Dog, City, Mistake*).

modal having to do with the way in which a clause meaning relates to truth or falsity: *may* is a modal **auxiliary verb** indicating that the rest of the clause is only supposed to be POSSIBLY true; *clearly* can serve as a modal adjunct indicating that the statement it introduces is OBVIOUSLY true.

modifier phrase which alters the meaning of a constituent without its presence being governed by some other item. The underlined parts of *Do it <u>on Tuesday</u>; I agree <u>emphatically</u>; the girl <u>with the dragon tattoo</u>; a <u>quiet</u> woman <u>who no one had noticed</u>.*

neuter belonging to the gender class that agrees with the pronoun *It* rather than *He* or *She.*

nominative the form for a pronoun that is the subject of a clause showing a **tense** contrast, e.g. *we* or *they.*

noun word of the class whose members often name types of things or stuff: *apple, mountain, gasoline.*

noun clause traditional name for some content clauses.

NP Noun Phrase: phrase with a noun as its **head**.

object an object is a constituent (almost always an **NP**) normally coming after the **verb** and denoting something immediately affected or connected. The underlined NP in VPs like *opened <u>a new bottle</u>*; *caused <u>trouble</u>*; *take <u>your time</u>*; *hand <u>the usher</u> <u>your ticket</u>*.

open interrogative   interrogative with a wide-open, indefinitely large range of potential answers, like *How often do you come here?*

participle   **verb** form not showing a **tense** contrast: the **past participle** *taken* or the **gerund-participle** *taking*.

particle   single-word unit (usually a **preposition**) which can appear either before the direct object (*pick <u>up</u> your shoes*) or after it (*pick your shoes <u>up</u>*).

passive   not of the active type. In a passive clause, the **verb** is in **past participle** form and its meaning has been flipped so that the two main NPs (usually the **subject** and the **object**) switch roles. The passive counterpart of *Your dog bit me* is *I was bitten by your dog*.

past   the tense used for referring to past time events, as in *I usually <u>walked</u>* or *It felt <u>damp</u>*, and in certain other ways (like the hypothetical sense in *if I <u>wanted</u> to*).

past participle   the form of the **verb** (often ending in *-ed* or *-en*) used after *Have* to form the **perfect** construction (*I have already <u>written</u> it*) or used in the **passive** (*The alligator was humanely <u>killed</u>*).

perfect   construction with **past participle** governed by *Have* to express completed action with present relevance, as in *has sung*.

person   the grammatical property that distinguishes between *us* (1st person: includes the utterer), *you* (2nd person: includes the addressee but not the utterer), and *them* (3rd person: includes neither).

plain form   the basic form of a **noun**, **verb**, or **adjective** without any suffixes added: *be, do, make,* etc.

plural   referring to some number other than one of what some noun denotes, as in *apples*.

possessive   see **genitive**

PP Preposition Phrase: phrase with a **preposition** as its **head**.

preposition word of the category exemplified by *at, between, by, despite, into, of, throughout,* etc.

present the **tense** used for expressing either habitual practice throughout time, as in *I usually walk,* or present-moment time, as in *It feels damp.*

progressive construction with **gerund-participle** preceded by *Be* to express continuing activity, as in *is singing.*

pronoun member of a small subcategory of special nouns used to make a reference either to some NP nearby in the sentence or to something in the context: *He, I, It, One*$_{\text{pro}}$, *She, They, We, You*$_{\text{pl}}$, *You*$_{\text{sg}}$.

proper noun noun naming some specific identifiable person, place, thing, or creation: *Gandhi, Chicago, Kilimanjaro, Hamlet.*

reflexive pronoun pronoun word-form ending in *-self,* normally used for referring back to an NP in the same clause.

relative clause clause like *which frightened us* or *that nobody wanted,* most commonly used to modify a noun in an NP.

singular referring to just one of what some noun denotes, as in *apple.*

specifier (not used in this book – I've never been quite sure whether linguists who use it intend it to be a category name like **determinative** or a function name like **determiner**).

stranded of a **preposition**, separated from its understood complement, as in *Who did you see __?,* where *see* is understood as if it had *who* as its object.

subject the subject of a clause is the obligatory constituent (usually an **NP**) normally coming before the **VP**; the underlined parts of *Several of the members thought otherwise*; *Nobody does it better*; *Half past nine or a quarter to ten should work.*

subordinator word belonging to the tiny category including

Whether and **That**$_{sbr}$. [Many linguists call them "complementizers," but that's not a good choice of term, because a subordinator can introduce a relative clause, which is a **modifier**, as well as a **complement** clause.]

superlative   the version of an **adjective** or **adverb** that is used for the extreme of the scale: *highest, loudest, fastest, most.*

tense   the property of a **verb** that distinguishes *investigates* and *speaks* (current or habitual time reference) from *investigated* and *spoke* (past time reference).

verb   word of the category including *investigate, think, fondle, seem, bring.*

VP   Verb Phrase: phrase with a **verb** as its **head**.

wh-word   one of the set of words used to introduce relative or open interrogative clauses: *who, what, which, where, when, how, why.*

word   see the entries for **lexeme** and **word-form**.

word-form   particular shape of a word that can appear in a sentence: *take* or *takes* or *taken* or *taking.*

Index